Deer, Moose, Elk, and Their Family

TITLE-PAGE DRAWING: *Whitetail deer*

Deer, Moose, Elk, and Their Family

Marie M. Jenkins

drawings by Matthew Kalmenoff

HOLIDAY HOUSE · New York

DEDICATED TO MY NIECES,

JEANNE AND CAROLYN

Library of Congress Cataloging in Publication Data

Jenkins, Marie M. 1909-
  Deer, moose, elk, and their family.

  Includes index.
  SUMMARY: Introduces the large array of animals
belonging to the deer family, including the elk, sika,
moose, reindeer, and caribou.
  1. Cervidae—Juvenile literature. [1.Cervidae.
2. Deer] I. Kalmenoff, Matthew. II. Title.
QL737.U55J46   599'.7357   79-2111
ISBN 0-8234-0362-9

Contents

Acknowledgments

I wish to thank the librarians at James Madison University, Harrisonburg, Virginia; especially the Research Librarian, Tom McLaughlin, and Marcia Grimes, who was in charge of Loan Services. Both were most helpful in obtaining books and journals and in securing additional information when it was needed. Thanks are also due the librarians at Lord Fairfax Community College at Middletown, Virginia, who gave most willing assistance.

I also appreciate the special efforts of Dr. Chris Wemmer, Director of the National Zoological Park Conservation Center at Front Royal, Virginia; and Dr. Anton Bubenik of the Wildlife Branch Research Station, Ministry of Natural Resources, Maple, Ontario, Canada; and Dr. William Kemp of the Department of Endodontics at the Medical College of Virginia in Richmond, Virginia. These scientists assisted me greatly in obtaining information not otherwise available.

1
Majestic Giants of the Ice Age

Close to 250,000 years ago great herds of giant deer roamed the open "parkland" forests of Europe. They were stately creatures, with heads held high and wide-spreading antlers. The animals were so large that even a very tall person would not have been able to see over a big stag's shoulder.

Antlers of the giant deer were enormous. The beams, or main shafts, stretched out on either side, then each one flattened into a broad plate with half a dozen large tines jutting up along the front edge. They looked somewhat like the antlers of a bull moose, except that a moose's antlers are much smaller, and the platelike areas are held more or less parallel to the ground. In the giant deer the whole plate is tilted upward almost at a right angle. This causes the big tines along its front rim to curve inward and backward over the deer's head and back.

No other animal has ever had such large antlers as the giant deer. Two men standing with arms outstretched and only their fingertips touching could hardly have reached from one tip to the other of these great antlers. According to a widely accepted book of animal records, the largest set ever found measured four and a quarter meters across, and that is almost 14 feet.

For well over 200,000 years giant deer lived all across northern Europe and Asia. Again and again great glaciers crept down from the north, thick enough to ride over and cover even the tallest trees with a sheet of ice. As they moved slowly on, year by year, deer and other animals headed southward.

Each cold period lasted for hundreds or thousands of years. During this time millions of tons of water were locked in the great ice sheets. The ocean level was lowered over all the earth, and much shallow sea bottom was left bare. What we now call the British Isles became a part of the European mainland, and there was no English Channel or Irish Sea. Giant deer and other creatures wandered into these western lands and made their home there.

In between the cold periods were long spans of time when the ice melted back and the climate turned warmer. Trees and other plants grew again, and animals spread northward. The sea level rose, and the land bridges disappeared.

Giant Deer and Early Humans

Prehistoric people lived on the continent of Europe during the later glacial periods. They hunted the great deer for food, and probably also for clothing. Bones of early men and women and of giant deer have been found together in riverbed and cave deposits. Sometimes bone or flint tools have been found also. Some of the long bones of the deer were split as if they had been opened with a sharp instrument so the marrow could be taken out. One big deer skull had a deep cut in its forehead of the right size and shape to have been made by a hatchet. Other long bones look as if they had been used for hammer-stones.

Giant deer were also used as models for some of the earliest cave paintings. In the Cougnac cave in Dordogne, France, is a painting of several of these animals. With their enormous platelike antlers tilted upward they cannot be mistaken for any other kind of creature. Because of their antlers, scientists have given them the name *Megaceros giganteus*. The two words mean "great-horned giant."

The "Irish Elk"

No one knows just when giant deer finally reached Ireland, but there is probably not a county in the country where its bones have not been found. In some places remains of a hundred or more have turned up at one spot, just as if a whole herd had perished at one time. Larger skeletons and antlers have been found in Ireland than in any other country. Several of the skeletons are nearly perfect, with few or no missing parts.

Most of Ireland's museums have more than one skeleton, and they often have many pairs of the wide-spreading antlers. Other skeletons, or skulls and antlers, have been sent to museums in different countries. The largest set of antlers in the United States is at Yale University.

These fossil antlers have long been common in the Irish countryside. Some families have put them up in their homes as ornaments; others hung clothes on them. Outside, the antlers were used for such things as gateposts. No other animal that the people knew of had unusually large antlers except the European elk. Soon the giant deer became known as the "Irish elk." This is a poor name for it, however, for no elk ever had antlers shaped like these. Also, the giant deer is little more Irish than it is French, German, Italian, or Russian. Its remains are plentiful in all these countries.

So many farmers found both bones and antlers of giant deer when they were digging peat that many have mistakenly thought the animals usually died in peat bogs. The truth of the matter is that many of the animals, thousands of years earlier, died in lakes. Perhaps they were mired in mud or water plants, or they might have crashed through winter ice and drowned. Weighed down with heavy antlers, it would not be easy for them to get out again if they were caught. As hundreds of years passed the bones became covered with dirt and other materials that settled to the bottom. The bones themselves hardened into fossils. Finally, perhaps thousands of years later, the lakes filled up and were gradually changed into peat bogs. The bones and antlers were really in the chalky or limy clay at the bottom.

The last of the giant deer in eastern Europe died about 50,000 years ago, before the end of the Ice Age. In western Europe, and in Ireland, the great creatures continued to live on until the last big glacier had melted back toward the north. They became extinct only about 10,000 years ago.

Other Ancient Deer

Savin's giant deer (*Megaceros savini*), another member of this group, was probably an ancestor of the other giant deer. It appeared in Europe during the growth of some of the earliest glaciers, close to 500,000 years ago, and died out about the time the true giants arrived.

Savin's deer are a little smaller, and the antlers are not palmate—that is, they do not spread out to form flattened plates with tines around the rim. True palmate antlers somewhat resemble the palm of the hand with the tines sticking out like fingers. Antlers and skeletons of both these deer have been found all the way from Russia to the British Isles.

The earliest known member of the giant deer group appeared a little over a million years ago, during the time of the first glaciers of the Ice Age, and died out about the same time as Savin's deer. This animal was given the name of *verticornis* or "turned horn" deer (*Praemegaceros verticornis*) because of its peculiar antlers. The main beams grew almost straight outward, then turned upward, and did not become palmate except at the very tip.

The bush-antlered deer (*Eucladoceros dicranios*), another early member of this family, also had unusual antlers. Each one branched and rebranched until there were about twelve tines on each side. The tines were long and thick, and gave the big headpiece a tangled, bushy appearance.

Antlers Are Not Horns

Antlers are the one main distinguishing characteristic of the deer family. If an animal has antlers it has to be a deer, because no other kind of animal ever has this special kind of structure on its head. Horns are sometimes mistaken for antlers, but the two are completely different.

A horn is a hollow covering over a somewhat cone-shaped bony core. As long as the animal lives, this core continues to grow slowly, so long as the horn is not cut or broken off. The horny, hollow covering that fits over the bone is made of the same kind of material as claws, hair, hoofs, and fingernails. This covering—called keratin—is not alive, but it grows from the base much as fingernails do. Living cells in the skin make new cells. These push the older ones away, and they die. If a horn is cut off, the missing part can never grow again, any more than a new foot could grow if the end of the leg were cut off; the action is too disturbing to the core.

Horns are found in many creatures, from some of the dinosaurs to today's cattle, antelopes, and goats. They are at least 100 million years old. Unlike antlers, horns do not branch.

An antler is true bone. It grows by the action of bone-forming cells, just as any other bone does, although it grows extraordinarily fast. At its base is a pedicel, or short stalk of skull bone, on which the antler grows. The stalk contains blood vessels and is covered with tender, hairy skin called "velvet."

In most deer the growth of new antlers begins in early spring. A bony knob covered with velvety skin starts to develop on the pedicel. The first branch forms within about two weeks. By September the velvet-covered antlers are fully grown. Bone cells at the base, where the antler is connected to the stalk, now change their growth pattern. The flow of blood is cut off, first to the bone of the antlers, then to the velvet covering. Soon the velvet dries up and begins to peel off in ragged shreds. Perhaps this peeling causes the velvet to itch a great deal, for a deer continually rubs them against branches and bushes. Sometimes he even eats a piece that hangs down in his way. A few days later all the dried skin is gone.

The hard, bony antlers now have neither blood supply nor nerves, and can no more feel pain than can hair or the tips of the fingernails. Soon after the antlers are hardened, male deer become very aggressive. They begin to court the females and to fight off any other males that try to interfere with their courtship.

From left to right we see the antlers of a mule deer just starting to grow in February; developing further in April; pronged and covered with velvet in June; shedding their velvet in August; and fully grown in October. Below is a cross-section of a developing antler, showing the growing bone inside and the coating of velvet on the outside.

Fallen Antlers

In late fall or early winter, after the courtship days are over, some of the cement that holds the antler to the pedicel is absorbed by the deer's body. This leaves a weak spot. When the antler now happens to strike a tree branch or other object it is knocked off cleanly, much as a hat might be nudged from one's head.

Fallen antlers are a boon to small creatures such as mice, porcupines, and squirrels. They gnaw on the pieces, breaking them up, and swallow the fragments. These are a good source of salt and calcium, or lime. In some places where the soil is poor, deer also eat pieces of cast antlers. One naturalist saw a female chewing on a male's antlers while they were still on his head.

No scar tissue forms when an antler is shed. Instead, a new growth of hairy velvet quickly covers the stalk, then all the cells there go into a resting period. This dormant stage lasts until early spring. Then the process of growing new antlers begins all over again.

Early humans made much use of cast antlers. Neanderthals, who lived in Europe 35,000 to 100,000 years ago, used the antlers for weapons such as spear points or handles for stone tools. Later the Cro-Magnon people, who lived until about 10 or 12 thousand years ago, fashioned pieces of antler into such tools as barbed harpoon tips, and polished needles that were used to sew skins together.

Sometimes the antlers had pictures scratched onto them. One small piece about 15,000 years old shows a bison licking its back. Coarse hair on the brow and soft fur on the muzzle can be seen. On another longer piece about the same age, a very natural-looking horse is achieved by following the antler's shape; the animal seems to be leaping away from the antler into the air.

Except for a developing embryo, antlers grow far faster than any other kind of living tissue. Some years ago a medical student made a microscope slide of a growing antler and showed it to one of his professors without telling him what it was. The professor, Dr. James Ewing, was a cancer specialist. When he examined the slide he said it looked exactly like malignant bone cancer.

Since then the young student, now Dr. Walter Modell, has tried to find what sort of mechanism controls the fierce growth of antler cells. He wants to know how such fast growth can be stopped, as well as started. Other scientists have studied this too but, so far, it is still a mystery.

Squirrels and other small animals nibble on the shed antlers of moose, as shown, and other deer, thus adding to the minerals needed by their bodies.

It is remarkable that so much bone can grow in so short a time, for antlers can be quite heavy. Those of Megaceros, the giant deer, weigh about the same as three or four heavy typewriters, or from 30 to 45 kilograms (about 66-99 pounds). This is more than the weight of all the rest of the skeleton.

Deer Are Mammals

Like all other mammals, female deer have mammary, or milk, glands, and nurse their young. These glands are the reason the name "mammal" was chosen for this class. Most deer have four nipples, just as cows do, located close to the hind legs. Baby deer, or fawns, get up on wobbly legs soon after they are born and nurse while standing. They nudge and butt the mothers' udders with small noses in their haste to get a stomach full of milk.

All mammals, even whales and elephants, have hair or fur at least some time in their lives. They also are warm-blooded, and can control the body temperature, often by means of sweat glands just below the surface of the skin. When an animal becomes too warm, little droplets of sweat ooze out. These evaporate from the heat from the body, and this cools the skin.

Animals with much thick hair often have only a few sweat glands, or none at all. In deer the sweat glands are on the muzzle near the mouth, in the skin between the toes, and in the area of skin at the base of the tail. During the winter a deer's furry coat traps air close to the body, where it is warmed by body heat. This trapped layer insulates the body and keeps it warm.

Nearly all deer have facial glands. These are located in

two pits, one in front of each eye, that are lined with body skin. Deer may also have other skin glands on the forehead or other parts of the face, near the tail, or on the legs.

All mammals have specialized teeth. These are of four kinds: the front or biting teeth, called incisors; the canines or dog teeth, which are usually cone-shaped; and two kinds of cheek teeth, the premolars and molars. In deer the two canine teeth in the lower jaw, one on each side, look just like the biting teeth and lie close to them. The upper jaw has no biting teeth at all, and usually no canines. Instead there is a horny pad over the gums that the lower teeth press against.

Food and Feeding

Most deer are browsers, and are more likely to eat twigs than grass. They twist their rough tongues around a piece of plant, then clamp down on it and jerk off a mouthful. This is swallowed whole with little or no chewing.

Deer are cud-chewers, or ruminants, as are sheep, goats, cattle, and antelopes. These animals are peculiar in that they have four "stomachs" instead of one. The first is a big pouch called the rumen where swallowed food is stored. Next to it is a much smaller honeycomb stomach lined with shallow pits. Microscopic organisms act on food in the large pouch and start it to fermenting. After a while the food, which by now is partly digested and rather slimy, is passed on to the second stomach where more digestion and fermentation take place. Later, when the deer is ready to stop eating and rest, it brings a ball of this food up again into its mouth from the second chamber.

The food is now thoroughly chewed and mixed with

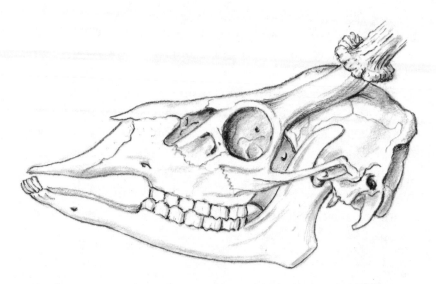

The heavy, somewhat squarish cheek teeth of a deer are efficient mashers of tough plant food, as seen in this mule-deer skull. The narrower incisor teeth at the front, flanked by the canines, are adapted for grasping tree bark and grasses. Note the base of the antler at the rear of the skull.

saliva. Ridges of hard enamel on the cheek teeth of deer can rasp and break up almost any kind of hard plant material. When the food is swallowed a second time, another mouthful is brought up. The chewed food is further digested in the third and fourth chambers, then it is passed to the intestines, where digestion is completed.

Running Mammals with Hoofs

All deer have feet and legs that are especially adapted for running. They walk on the toe tips, with ankles and heels held so high above the ground that they look like the lowest joints of the legs. The first digit of each foot, the "thumb," or big toe, has disappeared completely. Second and fifth toes are usually quite small and rarely touch the ground.

The weight of the animal is borne by the third and fourth toes. Foot bones, or those that reach between the toes and the ankle or heel, are grown together and form one long bone, the cannon bone. Each of the third and fourth toes ends in a hoof, which is much like a thick, heavy, overgrown toenail.

All animals that have hoofs are known as ungulates. Those that bear the weight of the body on a very large middle or third toe, such as horses, are said to be odd-toed. Deer and other animals with two hoofs on each foot are called even-toed ungulates. The scientific term for this group is artiodactyls.

Pigs and hippopotamuses are artiodactyls, but they do not chew a cud. Ruminants, or true cud-chewers, include the deer family, or Cervidae; the giraffes; the pronghorns of North America; and all the hollow-horned creatures such as cattle, antelopes, and goats. All have four-chambered stomachs.

Two other groups chew a cud, but are not true ruminants because the third stomach is not developed. The fourth chamber, or true stomach, is always present. This is where digestive enzymes are made, the chemicals that aid in digesting food. Camels, llamas, and their relatives form one family of nonruminants. The other is the traguline family, or mouse deer. These creatures are about the size of a rabbit or small dog, and are found mainly in Africa and southeast Asia.

Pointed snouts cause mouse deer to look a good deal like large rats with slender legs and hoofs. These animals have no facial glands and no antlers. Canine teeth are in the upper jaw and in the males these grow to be long, sharp tusks that curve down over the lower lip. All four toes are well developed on each foot, although the second and fifth ones are shorter and end in structures that look more like claws than hoofs. These are called false claws or pseudoclaws.

Mouse deer are thought to be very much like the early ancestors of even-toed hoofed mammals. Their earliest fossils are about 50 million years old and are known mainly from Asia.

Early Beginnings

The earliest antlered deer known is Dicrocerus, the forked-horn deer. These animals were small and the antlers simple, with only one fork. They first appeared in Europe about 25 million years ago. Forked-horn deer must have been quite hardy for they did not die out until almost three million years ago, close to the time the Pleistocene, or Ice Age, started.

Since the oldest and most primitive deer fossils have been found in Asia, it is probable that the deer family had its beginnings there. During millions of years these early forms spread not only throughout Europe, but a few wandered into the northern part of Africa. No deer fossils have ever been found in central or southern Africa, so it is likely that deer never lived there.

Other deer roamed northward and eastward, and finally reached North America. Some of our deer are almost exactly like certain deer in Europe. Land animals could not walk from Siberia to Alaska today because a wide body of water, Bering Strait, separates the two shores. Several times, however, there has been a land connection between Asia and

North America, especially when the enormous glaciers formed.

Sometimes this great land bridge, called Beringia, was almost as broad as Alaska itself. Each time it lasted for hundreds or thousands of years. Many creatures besides deer crossed over to this part of the world, and a number of North American mammals went from our continent to Asia.

During these long periods of time different groups of deer in both Eurasia and North America met all sorts of climates. They needed to be able to live in many kinds of places, from rocky or tree-covered mountains to river valleys or grasslands or dry prairie. Some could not adapt to such changed conditions and, little by little, these groups died out. Others were able to change. Their bodies could fit in wherever they had to live. Instead of dying out they evolved into the many different kinds of deer that we have today.

2

The Red Deer of Kings and the Wapiti of Commoners

European red deer (*Cervus elaphus*) are the most typical representatives of the deer family. *Elaphus* is a Greek word for "deer" and *cervus* is a Latin word meaning "like a deer." There are many races, or subspecies, of red deer, and they are found not only in Europe but scattered throughout Asia and even into northern Africa. None occurs in Australia, but races of red deer, called by another name, have also ranged over much of North America.

Red deer were important in the diet of prehistoric people in Europe as long as 400,000 years ago. Beginning about 12,000 years back, bones of red deer were more common in the midden heaps, or piles of "kitchen" scraps, than those of any other animal. Reindeer were used nearly as often.

Thousands of years later, when Europe was carved up into kingdoms, red deer came to be reserved for the "sport" of the nobility. Up until the French Revolution, in the last quarter of the eighteenth century, these animals could be hunted only by kings and nobles. Any commoner who dared to kill one for food was severely punished.

V.I.P. Deer

Because of the importance of red deer, certain terms came into use. A female is usually called a doe, but the European red deer female was known as a hind. Male red deer became "stags" instead of "bucks" and an older stag with large antlers was a "hart."

Even the tines on the antlers were given special names. The first tine, near the base, is a "brow tine." The second is a "bez" and the third, still farther up, is a "trez." In young stags the tip is usually forked but antlers of mature males develop three tines at the end. These three in red deer form a crown, or cup. A hart with three prongs on the main beam and a crown at the tip is a "twelve-pointer" or a "royal."

European red deer are larger and heavier than the average mule deer or Virginia whitetail of North America. The different subspecies vary much in size, but this seems to depend a great deal on where they live and how much nourishing food they can obtain. Red deer in Europe usually live in open forest and parkland and, like most deer, browse on the tender shoots, twigs, and leaves of trees and shrubs. They do not do as well when forced to eat chiefly grass.

Deer in the British Isles live mainly on heaths and moors where there is little browse, and are noticeably smaller than parkland deer. In the nineteenth century a herd of small-sized Scottish deer was taken to South Island, New Zealand, and set free. The idea was to provide both "sport" and fresh meat, for no large animals are native to this country. Within 20 years the descendants weighed twice as much as the deer first brought in, and some stags had 20-point antlers.

In the following years other groups were brought in. They flourished and grew in numbers until they became pests, and in 1930 had to be put under strict government control. They had damaged farm crops, eaten and trampled native plants, and overgrazed high mountain pastures so much that big gullies were eroded. As a result, water needed for industry and farms was lost because it ran off too quickly to be saved for later use. Now great numbers of deer are

killed each year, and the meat and hides sold for millions of dollars.

European red deer are a reddish-brown color, sometimes even golden-red, with white underparts and a yellowish-white rump patch. The winter coat has a brownish-gray tinge and the males grow a thick, dark mane on the underside of the neck. Hinds are about a third smaller than the males, and are lighter in color.

Red Deer Herds

Stags and hinds live separately most of the year. Males either live alone or form small groups of only a few animals. These change often as one leaves and another joins. No male is head or chief over the others.

Hind groups are large, perhaps up to several dozen. An older, mature female, usually with one or two offspring at her side, is the leader, and all follow her direction. Deer stalkers have given her the nickname "herself of the long neck," because she so constantly raises her head to watch out for any danger to the herd. Other hinds take turns at being "smeller-hearer-watcher" but the leader is always the most alert.

If anything happens to alarm the herd, the hind that first discovers the trouble raises her head and gives a short, sharp, loud bark. All deer within hearing take notice. If the disturbance continues the leader guides the herd away. They move silently, often stopping for an instant to look back. At each stop the leader gives a sharp warning bark.

A family of European red deer, Cervus elaphus. *They are bigger than the average American whitetail or mule deer.*

Young deer of both sexes stay with the hinds until they are about three years old. In early summer the hinds that are carrying young leave the herd, one by one, when it is nearing time for the fawns to be born. Each hind is followed by her own offspring, but when the fawn is born she drives them off.

Three-year-old males leave the herd for good at this time, and join other young males. Some two-year-olds may go also. The yearlings seem to think that being chased off is play and pester the mother, running back again and again. As soon as the hind allows it they and most of the two-year-olds return to stay. The yearling will sometimes nurse, along with the new offspring, for several weeks longer.

A fawn is left alone for the first few days, but the mother returns to feed it about twice a day. Newborn deer have no odor at this time, and their dappled hair blends in so well with the sun and shade around them that one almost has to be stepped on before it can be seen. Unless a fawn moves, enemies are not likely to find it.

The First Summer

Mammals have larger and better-developed brains than other animals, and are more intelligent. Perhaps it is as a result of this that young mammals of all kinds play a great deal. Deer are no exception. Not only do they run and leap and kick up their heels, but they often seem to be playing games.

Young deer follow a leader in single file, much as children do, or one may run madly after another until he tags it and runs off, with the other now at his heels. Sometimes one youngster chasing another around a hillock will suddenly turn and gallop in the opposite direction, catching the other by surprise. The second one is likely to pop up its ears, jump stiff-legged into the air, then wheel around and dash back the way it came. The next time it is ready for this trick, or may give it a try itself.

Most games last only a few minutes, and hinds often join in. Young stags, however, soon become more interested in mock fights than in games. With heads low and small antlers together they turn this way and that, and push and shove. Full-grown stags rarely play although, as the mating season nears, one may pretend to jab his antlers into his neighbor's side in a playful manner.

Mating Calls

In early fall, when the velvet is gone and the antlers hardened, stags begin to come together in small bands. Instead of walking they now tend to trot stiff-legged. About two weeks before the rut, or mating season, starts they hunt out old wallows.

These are boggy places the stags churn with their feet until the water sometimes becomes like a thick liquid. The areas may be large enough for two or three stags to roll in at the same time. They wallow here once or twice a day, becoming caked with mud, until the rut is over. Hinds often lie down and roll in clear water, but do not use the wallows made by stags.

During most of the year the stag is silent, but his larynx, or voice box, develops more after the antlers grow. All during the rutting season he can be heard giving forth a loud, growling roar which announces to all the world that he is ready for mating. A month and a half later, when the rut is over, he gives voice to only a low moan.

As the rut begins, the glands in front of the stag's eyes secrete a yellowish, waxy liquid that oozes out and dries on his face, giving him a strong, musky odor. His neck swells and he struts about, antlers held high. Only one thing interests him now: seeking females. Food is forgotten. Boldly he pushes into the hinds' territory, cocky and ready at any instant to start a fight.

The stag soon rounds up a group of hinds, herding them to one side in as large an area as he can defend. He may have half a dozen, or 50 or more, depending on how many stags nearby are also trying to gather a company of females. For the next few days he runs around his group continuously, roaring every few minutes, pawing the ground with his forefeet, or showing off his antlers. He may lie down at times, but the instant another stag comes too close he jumps to his feet and is on the run again.

Rivals Clash

Smaller stags in rut may stand and bellow, but rarely try to interfere. Another large stag in rut, however, is a different matter. He may try to drive off a few hinds, or challenge the master of the herd. In either case a fight is likely to follow.

Antlers are mainly weapons for sparring, not for killing. The two stags stand head to head, antlers together, and push and shove with all their strength. The idea is to get past the other's defenses and lunge a broadside into his ribs. Sooner or later one will give in and trot off. The winner roars his victory, then turns to herding the hinds that have not wandered off or been stolen while the fighters were busy.

Once in a while a deer is gored by an antler, especially a broken one, and is wounded or killed, but this is not common. Also, antlers sometimes become locked together and the stags cannot pull themselves apart no matter how hard they struggle. When this happens both animals die a miserable death by starvation.

In between roaring and herding his hinds the stag attempts to mate with one or another of the females. Often she runs off. He may follow, or turn his attention to another hind nearby. While this goes on he must at the same time keep a close watch on the whole group, or a rival may make away with some of his mates.

After a few days the herd master is exhausted. He leaves his group and goes off by himself for a day or two of rest. When he comes back it is usually to find his females have been corralled or stolen by one or more other stags. Fit and rested, he roars his challenge. Males that have been with hind groups are now likely to be weary, and in a short time he will have won one or more fights, and rounded up a group again.

For the most part the hinds pay little attention to what goes on. They feed, or lie quietly and chew their cuds. Whether herded by one stag or another, they seem to be content.

Groups of females herded by a male are commonly called harems, but there is a question as to whether this term can properly be used with deer. A true harem master is the leader of the group. He not only drives away males and mates with the females, but he also protects all the group against any danger. If a deer herd is alarmed, however, the hinds ordinarily follow their usual leader, a female, and pay little attention to the herd master. He may stay with the group but he is much more likely to go charging off on his own, and return only when all danger is past.

The mating period in many wild animals comes at a certain time of the year. Breeding takes place in most cases when there is some kind of change in the daily amount of light. In the springtime, for example, there is a little more light day by day, but in the fall the days grow shorter. The light signal for red deer is the day in mid-September when the sun shines for less than twelve hours and fourteen minutes. As soon as this happens, and the temperature falls, changes begin in red deers' bodies. Before long they are ready to mate.

By the time the rut is over, six or seven weeks later, snows and blizzards and the cold of winter have usually arrived. Many of the older, worn-out stags die, especially if the winter is harsh and the food scarce. The weak, the old, and up to half the young ones are likely to die before the following spring. This is nature's way of taking care of the unfit. The healthiest and strongest animals live, and this is best for the herd.

Red deer are thought to live, on the average, about 15 years, but those that are well cared for in zoos may live much longer. Several have lived to be over 20, but the record is held by a red deer at the National Zoo in Washington, D.C. It died on March 24, 1941, having lived 26 years, six months, and two days after its arrival at the zoo.

Beringia, the Land Bridge

The oldest fossils we have found of red deer in Europe and Asia date back about half a million years ago. It was much later that red deer pushed to the north and east. Some of them finally reached the far northeast tip of what is now Siberia and found their way across Beringia, the great land bridge.

Scientists are not sure exactly when this migration to North America took place, because they have not yet been able to study enough fossils from different places. We know the animals came to our continent at least 100,000 years ago, and it might have been as long ago as 250,000 years. This would place the migration either shortly after or before one of the last great glaciers. It is possible that different groups came at both times. We do know that red deer would not have crossed Beringia during the coldest period, because they are not arctic animals.

Red deer thrived in North America. During the thousands of years that followed their arrival they spread south and east until they reached what is now Mexico, and almost to the Atlantic Ocean. There was plenty of food and the animals grew to be quite large.

Wapiti—the So-Called Elk

Big male red deer in North America were about the size of today's saddle horses, and their magnificent antlers spread almost as wide as the animals were tall. They had light yellowish rump patches that looked white against their rich, dark, reddish-brown fur. Because of the pale rump patch, Shawnee Indians, centuries later, gave the animals a name that most zoologists use today. It is "wapiti," or "white hair." The scientific name is *Cervus elaphus canadensis*.

When early English colonists first saw this deer they were amazed. It was so much larger than their own deer back home that its size could be compared only to that of

The wapiti is a sturdily built animal that can stand off even such a danger as a pack of gray wolves.

the great elk of Europe. The colonists paid no attention to the fact that the European elk was hump-shouldered and donkey-eared, or that his antlers were broad and flattened, and a long flap of skin hung below his throat. It was size that mattered.

The name "elk" stuck. The wapiti, a true red deer, is now known all over North America as an elk. To distinguish it from the true elk of Europe it is often called the American elk. This mix-up causes even more confusion when we realize that North America does have a true elk, and that we call it by still another name.

Wapitis, or American elks, are long-legged, strong, and sturdy. Their great antlers have long beams that sweep outward and upward, then back over the shoulders. In the fall the hardened antlers are a rich brown with ivory-colored points, and look as if they are polished. Four tines on the beam curve forward and upward. The fourth, or royal, is the longest, stoutest, and deadliest. It is sometimes called the dagger-point tine. Wapitis rarely have cups or crowns.

Both males and females have large upper canines called elk tusks. For many years these teeth were in great demand as symbols of a fraternal order, and sold for as much as $75 a pair. Animals were slaughtered for the two teeth alone, and the carcasses left to rot.

Wild Bugles

Wapiti herds are much like those of European red deer. In the fall, when the rut begins, males thresh bushes with their antlers and roll in urine-soaked wallows; the odor of urine seems to be important in some way at this time. The males follow the females with neck outstretched, muzzle raised, and upper lip curled back. When wapitis fight they often rise on their hind legs and try to stab each other with the forefeet. These flying hoofs can be deadly weapons.

Instead of roaring, wapitis bugle their challenge to other males. The mating call starts as a low, chesty growl,

A wapiti's mating call is sometimes called "bugling" because part of it resembles the tones of that instrument. The call is a very impressive sound that is at the same time a challenge to any other male in the area.

then rises to a high, clear bugle tone that sounds much like a yodel. It ends sharply with a few coughing grunts. Some naturalists have termed this trumpeting call one of the most stirring sounds in nature.

After the rutting season is over, wapitis form large herds of both sexes with the leader a female. The animals spend the winter on wind-blown slopes as much as possible. They browse on tender twigs and leaves or paw through snow to reach grass and other plants beneath. If food is scarce the deer turn to bark, and strip some of the trees as high as they can reach.

As late as 1850 wapitis roamed over both plains and forests of the United States and southern Canada. Twenty years later none were left on the plains and by the turn of the century the animals had also disappeared from most of the southwest. Some were shot for food by pioneers struggling westward, but many were killed for "fun." Others were sold for meat or were simply forced off the land because it was taken over for ranches, farms, and cities.

Today wapitis live mainly in reserves such as Yellowstone National Park, where they are protected. When snows are deep in winter, game wardens bring hay and salt blocks to the animals, using airplanes or special trucks. What the animals really need, however, is enough native vegetation, left where it is growing.

Hunting for food and eating natural food keeps the herd in better health. It also helps weed out the sick and unfit that cannot care for themselves. A good home for the animals would also have on it predators such as mountain lions and coyotes. Animals that kill for food choose the weakest first because they are easiest to get. Under these conditions both predators and prey would have plenty of food and would be much better off than when managed by humans. If we leave nature alone, it has a remarkable way of balancing itself.

Other Wapitis

Six races, or subspecies, of American wapitis are known, although two are now extinct. The Arizona, or Merriam, elk died out about 1900 and the eastern wapitis even earlier. The Manitoba elk, a prairie form, is now found only in Canada but earlier it ranged far down in the plains states.

The Roosevelt, or Olympic, wapiti is the largest race, but only a few thousand are left. They live on Vancouver Island in Canada and the Olympic Peninsula in Washington state. These animals have thick antlers that often have crowns toward the tip, much like those of European red deer.

Probably best known are the Rocky Mountain elk. They are almost as large as the Roosevelt wapitis, but are paler in color and have more slender antlers. Pockets of these animals live in the Rocky Mountains in both Canada and the United States. Their population today numbers about a million, and Rocky Mountain wapitis are in no danger of becoming extinct at present. In fact, they are so fertile and multiply so fast that hunters can get licenses to shoot about 10 per cent of the herds each year. The license fees are used for state and federal game-management programs such as bringing hay to the animals in winter. If all were allowed to live there would not be enough food, and most of them would starve.

Wapitis from the Rocky Mountain race have been used to restock a number of areas where the animals had been killed off years ago either by overhunting or because the places where they lived had been destroyed. In 1917, for example, two dozen elk from the Yellowstone National Park were released in the Jefferson National Forest in Virginia. They prospered in their new home and now several dozen roam freely in the Blue Ridge mountains.

The last of the six races, the tule or California elk, is the smallest. These animals are only about half as heavy as the Roosevelt wapitis and are often called dwarf elk. Not long after the gold rush began in the mid-19th century tule elk were almost wiped out. Hungry gold seekers needed food, and fresh elk meat brought good prices. By 1870 only one small band of a little over two dozen animals remained.

These were discovered hiding in a tule or bulrush marsh on the large Miller ranch in the San Joaquin valley. The owner promptly gave orders that the tule elk, as he called them, were to be protected, and posted a $500 reward for information about anyone that disturbed them. The small herd grew and soon became known as tule elk instead of dwarf elk. There are now about 700 of them scattered in three or four herds in California. Although not now in danger of becoming extinct, they still need protection. Farmers and ranchers who lease public lands for thousands of head of stock complain that the tule elk take food needed for domestic animals. These elk will not really be out of danger until a permanent home is set aside for them.

Conservationists who banded together to try to save these small creatures have had some success. In 1976 President Ford signed into law a bill stating none could be culled (killed because they were "extras") until the herds numbered 2000. Several have tried to bypass this law with one excuse or another but, so far, the dwarf elk are safe.

3

Sambars, Sikas, and Such

Nearly four centuries before Christ was born, Alexander the Great conquered most of the land from ancient Greece to India. On his return from these wars he brought back some large, rather unusual deer. They were sambars, members of one of the races of red deer in Asia. The deer were later examined by Aristotle. He was a famous philosopher and zoologist, and was the young Alexander's teacher. Aristotle told about these deer from India in his book *History of Nature.* In describing the antlers he said each one had only three tines. One at the base pointed forward and the tip was forked.

Many who had not seen the deer did not quite believe Aristotle. As the years passed these odd deer were almost forgotten but, centuries later, when they were again discovered in India, Aristotle was proved right. As a result the South Indian sambar (*Cervus [Rusa] unicolor niger*) is also known as Aristotle's deer.

Tens of thousands of years ago red deer in Asia spread out into such a variety of places to live that they finally developed into many different races. These can be gathered into five natural groups, each somewhat different from the other. Scientists have given each group a special name.

Indian Sambars

Sambars make up one genus known as Rusa deer, after the Malayan word for "deer." The Indian sambar is *Cervus unicolor* but the name can be written *Cervus [Rusa] unicolor* to show that it belongs to the Rusa group. Sometimes just *Rusa unicolor* is used.

These animals are all "unicolored," or one color, with no light underparts. Even the rump patch is a rusty brown. Fawns are usually born without spots, although they may show faintly in some of the newborn animals.

The South Indian sambar is a variety that is so dark it is almost black. This is the subspecies that Alexander the Great discovered. The word *niger*, meaning "dark," in the scientific name shows what race it is.

Sambars are large, long-legged deer with thick, rough antlers. They are smaller than American wapitis but larger than Virginia whitetails or mule deer. Most have a long, coarse-haired, bushy tail; sambars brought to parks and zoos in England and America have sometimes been nicknamed "horse-tailed deer."

In India these animals live in all kinds of forests, from tropical rain forests to mountainous areas covered with evergreens. Many live where there are wet and dry seasons instead of summer and winter. As a result sambars are likely to shed their antlers almost any month in the year. Even when taken to zoological gardens in other countries, where winters are cold, the stags drop antlers at odd times. This has given rise to a report that sambars often keep the same set of antlers for two to four years.

Sambar herds are very small, rarely more than four or five deer. Often there is just the mother with one or two offspring. Because mating takes place at different times, fawns are born in almost any month.

Sambar stags have stamping grounds as well as wallowing places. These are bare spots, free of grass, that sometimes cover as large an area as a small house would. Fights often

The sambar of India is a dark animal with rough antlers containing only three tines each. The animals are only four or five feet high.

take place here. Stags challenge each other with a mating call that is a loud, metallic roar.

When sambars are in heat the face glands in front of the eyes open so widely the stags are sometimes called "four eyes." The smelly secretion from the glands is rubbed on tree branches and other objects. Stags in rut paw the ground with their forelegs then toss bunches of loose grass and dirt into the air with their antlers. Sometimes they "preach" by standing on the hind legs and prancing about for a few seconds.

During the early part of the rut, members of both sexes develop a "sore spot" in a small region on the underside of the neck, near its base. The hair falls out, the area becomes swollen and bloody looking, and a thin substance drips from the sore. This also is probably used by the stags for scent-marking.

Sambars are very alert and at the first sign of danger one will give a loud, ringing "ponk" that can be heard a great distance. Hunters call this "belling." Sometimes an alarmed deer will signal the others by giving a hissing snort and stamping its feet on the ground.

The smaller Sunda or island sambars live on Java, Timor, and other islands off the coast of southeast Asia. They have been severely hunted, almost to extinction, but have been set free in the wild in a number of foreign places, including South Australia and Madagascar. Not many are found in zoos.

Small Sikas

Sika deer make up the second large group. They are hardy animals and thrive where conditions are poor and food is scarce. Sikas live in far eastern Asia, from China and Siberia to Japan. Of seven races known, five are now either extinct or in danger of becoming so.

Probably best known are the Japanese sikas (*Cervus [Sika] nippon*), the smallest of the group. When measured at shoulder height the males stand only slightly taller than an ordinary table. Japanese sikas are reddish brown, spotted with white in summer. Male sikas usually have four points on each antler. In spite of their small size they sometimes have savage fights during the rut. The mating cry is a shrill whistle that rises almost to a scream, then ends in a low grunt.

A great number of Japanese sikas live in parks and temple areas. They are so tame they will eat rice cakes that visitors bring for them. Many Japanese consider the temple sikas to be sacred animals.

Three races of endangered sikas live in the People's Republic of China. The mandarin sika of North China is the largest although it is smaller than the Indian sambar. We do not know if any members of these three races are still living in the wild. There have been no reports about them for years and it is possible they are extinct.

In 1969 a pregnant Formosan sika doe was shot and killed. This was the last report for that race, and Formosan sikas have now been declared extinct in the wild. However, a number live in various zoos and several hundred are being raised on farms in Taiwan. Perhaps in the future, forested wild areas, well protected, can be set aside for them and some of the captive animals can be used to set up a wild herd again.

Sikas can be successfully raised in captivity and have been taken to many countries. A number have either escaped or been set free and herds of Japanese sikas now run wild in Europe, North America, and New Zealand. Five sikas were let loose on James Island in Chesapeake Bay in 1916 and now there are over 1000. These sikas have spread to other islands and also into Maryland.

Antlers for Medicine

Sikas, like other animals, have been pushed out of forests where they used to live because trees were cut down and the land taken over for domestic stock or for growing crops. In some places they have been killed by the hundreds not only for their meat but for the antlers, which are thought to have medicinal value. In the Oriental medicine trade especially high prices are paid for antlers in velvet. Because of this some of the endangered deer are now being raised on farms and a "crop" of antlers is harvested each year.

For centuries traders have bought and sold rhinoceros horns, "dragon" teeth, deer antlers, and other animal parts that have been dried and ground up. Buyers used these substances as remedies for various illnesses, or for love potions, but no one was ever able to prove that any of them really had an effect. Now the Academy of Science in Moscow reports that clinical tests have been run on people, using chemicals from dried antlers in velvet. They find that antlers do indeed contain hormones and other chemicals which can be used to heal wounds and to help relieve certain symptoms of old age.

Twelve-Tined Swamp Deer

Barasinghas, the third group of Asian red deer, are large, graceful animals about the size of sambars. They have smooth summer coats of golden brown with pale spots.

Antlers in velvet shade almost to a deep orange. In the winter the coat is a dull, grayish-brown. The word "barasingha" means "twelve-tined" but these animals may have a few less or a few more than that number. The antlers are unusual in that there are no tines for over half the total length.

Years ago barasinghas were found over most of central and northern India and in nearby regions. They lived in marshes and plains on either side of great rivers and for that reason are often called swamp deer. Now only a few scattered herds are left. The North Indian barasingha *Cervus* [*Rucervus*] *duvaucelli*) lives mainly along the Sarda River in high grass swamps and grasslands. Many of the animals have been killed by poachers and most of the land has been taken over for rice and sugar cane fields. Now the government is setting aside a few national parks and sanctuaries where the animals can be protected.

Barasingha stags do not round up a collection of females at breeding time, and do not drive other stags away. Instead these deer live in mixed herds most of the year and separate into small male and female groups only during a period of two or three months when the fawns are born. However, the stags wallow and fight and bugle as other stags do. The mating call is a two-toned ringing note repeated 10 or 20 times. One naturalist said it sounded like "uu-aa, uu-aa."

Brow-Antlered Deer

Eld's deer (*Cervus* [*Rucervus*] *eldi*) are smaller-sized barasinghas. They are often called brow-antlered deer because the brow tine sweeps forward in such a way that it makes a continuous curve with the backward-arching main beam.

The name of the barasingha means "twelve-tined," but actually the number often varies; this one has ten tines.

Manipur brow-antlered deer are among the rarest in the world. In 1960 there were about 100 animals but a 1975 census showed only 14 were left—five stags, six hinds, and three fawns. These lived in a wetland area in Manipur, India.

A last-minute attempt is being made to ward off their extinction. The deer were placed in a reserved forest where all disturbance, such as cultivating crops, can be kept out and laws protecting the animals are being enforced. Also, two pairs of Eld's deer have been sent from the Delhi zoo to join a captive hind and fawn so the herd can be built up.

The thamin is another race of brow-antlered deer that lives in Burma. These animals live in large herds and feed mainly on wild rice and other marsh plants. So much of the flood-plain land where they live has been swallowed up by agriculture that the deer have turned to helping "harvest" the farmers' crops. As a result they have been shot down by the score.

Some years ago, when only a few hundred were left, Burma passed strict laws for their protection. The laws were enforced and thamin herds now number well over 3000. The animals are considered to be out of danger.

Deer with White Faces

Thorold's deer, or white-lipped deer (*Cervus albirostris*), is in a group by itself. These are long-legged, sturdy animals with wide hoofs like those of oxen and well-developed false claws. The muzzle is pure white. Females have a tuft of hair between the ears.

White-lipped deer live in high mountain meadows above the tree line, and feed mainly on grass and herbs.

Years ago these animals could be found in both Tibet and China but native hunters have killed so many that they are now in need of special protection. A few have been bred in zoos in China but, so far as is known, none has ever been taken out of the country except for a pair presented to Sri Lanka in 1972.

Dwarfs and African Deer

The fifth and last group is composed of Cervus deer, those that are most like European red deer. One of them, the Barbary stag (*Cervus elaphus barbarus*), is unusual in that it is the only native deer in Africa. These animals once roamed over much of northern Africa and scattered groups lived as far south as the middle of the Sahara. Barbary stags have stocky bodies and reddish-brown coats that show a few pale spots. Usually only ten tines are on the antlers.

Barbary deer are now found in one small region on the border between Tunisia and Algeria, living in cork-oak and pine forest land. Approximately 400 were counted in 1972; 150 in Algeria and 250 in Tunisia. Laws to protect the deer from hunting and trading have not been very well enforced, but a wildlife preserve is planned for them in Algeria. So far as is known there are no plans for such an area in Tunisia, but this country does have a breeding herd of several dozen animals.

Another Cervus race, dwarf red deer (*Cervus elaphus corsicanus*), lives on the Mediterranean islands of Corsica and Sardinia, north of Tunisia. These are reddish-brown little deer with upswung antlers. Usually four or perhaps five points develop on each.

These small deer are almost extinct. In 1965 only five

could be found on Corsica and none has been seen in recent years. Several dozen remained in Sardinia, located in two or three herds, but laws protecting them have been ignored. There is hope the deer can still be saved if a new hunting law is strictly enforced, and hunters' associations cooperate with it.

False Wapitis

Several races of red deer in Asia are so much like the American wapiti that they, too, are called wapitis at times. Scientists are still not agreed on whether this is correct. Most think that the American elk is only a subspecies of red deer because the two can mate with each other and produce healthy, normal offspring that have some characteristics of each parent. The mating call of males that are born from these two kinds of deer is itself a cross between a wapiti's bugle and a red stag's roar. Scientists who believe the American elk is a separate species write the scientific name as *Cervus canadensis*. They argue there are many examples of different species being able to mate—lions and tigers, for example. If they are right, the large Bactrian deer (*Cervus elaphus bactrianus*) should be known as the Bactrian wapiti (*Cervus canadensis bactrianus*).

This deer from south central Asia is very much like the American wapiti in appearance except for a few pale spots on its back. It was on the endangered list for years, but herds have now been moved to new areas, often in reserves, where they are protected. Numbers have increased to several hundred and the race is almost out of danger.

Another Asian wapiti, the stately Kashmir stag, or hangul (*Cervus elaphus hanglu*), is found only in the Vale of Kashmir in northern India. This is mountain land covered mostly with evergreen forests. Laws to protect the animals have not been respected and in the 1970 census only about 150 could be accounted for.

A few sanctuaries have been set aside for hanguls, and the World Wildlife Fund, which does much to help endangered species all over the world, has suggested that the following things be done in cases like this: organize patrols to stop poaching; punish severely all poachers who are caught; stop the use of sanctuary land for agriculture; and educate the public, both adults and children, so they will better understand the great value of wildlife.

Some of the largest subspecies of Asian red deer are known as marals, the Siberian name for deer. These are huge, dark-coated animals almost as large as American wapitis and they have heavy, many-tined antlers. Unlike many other red deer in Asia, marals do not seem to be greatly endangered either from overhunting or from the land they live on being taken over for crops and farm stock. Some are raised on farms and others have been bred in zoos and game parks.

One race of marals lives in Siberia and Manchuria. Others are found as far south and west as northern Iran and Asia Minor. The Altai maral (*Cervus elaphus sibiricus*) of north central Asia is most like the American elk and is often called the Altai wapiti. Members of this race lived at the New York Zoological Garden as early as 1903. Nearly five years later one of the females mated with a Bactrian deer and gave birth to a very healthy hybrid of the two races. It was presented to the Duke of Bedford, in England, and lived to be over 20 years old.

4

Red Deer Relatives

One of the strangest deer on earth has a history that is almost as curious as the creature itself. For hundreds, perhaps thousands of years, a captive herd was kept hidden behind high walls in the Imperial Hunting Park a short distance south of Peking, China. Except for those who were allowed to enter the emperor's summer palace, few others even knew the animals existed.

Père Armand David often wondered what animals lived there. He was a French priest who had been sent as a missionary to China in 1861, but he was also a zoologist. Part of his job was to collect specimens of Chinese birds and mammals and send them back to the National Museum of Natural History in Paris. He took long hikes searching for specimens, but no one could—or would—tell him what kind of creatures were hidden behind the high walls.

One day in 1865 Père David found a hill of sand that workmen had left piled against the outside wall. No guards were in sight. He climbed up and looked over the wall. Passing in front of him was a herd of strange, long-tailed deer with peculiar antlers and long, narrow faces.

Père David wrote home of the discovery. He thought the animals might be some kind of reindeer, but had learned the Chinese called them *Ssu-pu-hsiang*, which means "four characters that do not fit together." They said the big animals had stag's antlers, cow's feet, a camel neck, and a donkey tail.

A few months later Père David was able to bribe the guards. One night they dropped over the wall to him the skeletons and skins of a male and a female deer. He sent these directly to the Paris Museum. In less than a year the newly discovered deer had a name, and the description was published. All Europe now knew about the odd Père David's deer (*Elaphurus davidianus*). Four years later Père David discovered another unusual animal, the giant panda.

Now that the secret was out, three living deer were presented, by royal order, to the French Ambassador in Peking. These died on the voyage to France, but others followed. Before the century was ended zoos in several European countries had groups of Père David's deer—but China had none.

A great flood had broken and washed away part of the high park wall. Many deer were drowned. Others escaped, only to be killed and eaten by starving peasants. A few were captured but these were killed six years later during the Boxer Rebellion, except for one animal. It finally died in the Peking Zoo.

Strange Deer in Europe

With the deer in China gone, zoo directors decided to put their scattered small groups together and form one breeding herd, so the species could be saved. The Duke of Bedford, in England, took charge. All the remaining Père David's deer were released on his large estate at Woburn Abbey where herds of sika, fallow, red, and other kinds of deer already lived.

Père David's deer thrived. Several hundred small groups now live in zoos in a dozen or more countries in different

Père David's deer have horselike tails and rather broad, flat hoofs that were probably originally adaptations for walking on soft, swampy ground.

parts of the world. Four of the animals arrived at the Bronx Zoo in New York City in 1946, the first to reach the United States. Five years later another group was sent to the Peking Zoo, where the last deer from the hidden herd had died so long ago.

Behavior Patterns

Scientists believe Père David's deer has been extinct in the wild for at least 3000 years. We know the animals once lived in both China and Japan, for their fossils have been found in both places. Probably they lived on swampy, reedy floodplains, for the long, broad hoofs look as if they were suited for walking in marshy places. When the animals walk on dry ground the hoofs often make a curious clicking sound.

These animals have lived only in captive herds for so many centuries that their behavior patterns may be quite different from those of other deer. One place this is being studied is at the Research and Conservation Center at Front Royal, Virginia. This is a branch of the National Zoological Park at Washington, D.C., where rare birds and mammals are raised and studied. Dr. Chris Wemmer, director of the center, is in charge of the work being done with Père David's deer.

Most of the research is carried on during the mating season from June to August. The males challenge each other with a loud *hong-g* that sounds much like a donkey's bray. In a fight they push, shove, bite, and rise on their hind legs to strike each other with sharp hoofs. The winner becomes herd master of the small group of females here. A week or two later, too droopy and tired to run off a rival, he may have to give up the females to a new herd master.

In the present research Dr. Wemmer and his assistants are trying to learn what kinds of signals the deer use to give information to or "talk" to other deer. They also want to know what effect other things such as the age of the animal, its body size or, in males, the shape and size of the antlers might have on the way each animal acts. For this work it is necessary to be able to tell exactly which animal is which, and not get them mixed up.

Females wear tags around their necks. Males are identified by their antlers. In these deer each antler branches once at the base to form two long beams. One goes almost straight up and forks at the tip while the other grows backward. This one does not fork, although in older deer small tines develop on it. Antlers on each deer are almost as individual as fingerprints.

A special study is made of antlers, for their size, shape, and condition can be very important in settling which buck will be the father of next year's fawns. Shed antlers are collected and weighed, and several measurements taken. Records are kept for each buck over a period of years, beginning when he is a yearling with spikes.

Importance of Research

The actions of each male animal are checked for several hours a day during the rutting season by a person especially assigned to him. In this way it is possible to find out, for each animal, such things as whether or not he is timid, mean, weak, strong, a bully, or a good leader. These facts are then checked with what has been learned about the antlers to see if there is any relationship.

Scientists and breeders want to know exactly how any one of these things influences a buck's behavior. They need answers to such questions as: Which male is herd master most often? For how long a time? Which one fights the most? How often does he win or lose? Which one is father of the most fawns? Is there any one buck the females will not accept? If so, why the rejection? What effect does age or antler size or any other factor have on all this?

After learning as many answers as possible the workers will try to choose which buck or bucks would be best for the herd. This buck should then be kept with the herd and not sent off for exhibit or display. Also, they want to see if any of this information can be used in breeding other species of deer, especially those that might be rare.

Research is never "trying to prove something." It is trying to discover some truth by asking endless questions about whatever the scientist is studying, and searching for correct answers. Then other people in all sorts of jobs may be able to put this knowledge to good use. In this case the research may help in saving some species from extinction.

Europe's Most Popular Deer

Fallow deer (*Dama dama*) have had a long history. Fossils a quarter of a million years old have been found from southeastern Asia to as far north as Denmark. These early fallow deer, known as Clacton deer, were large and strong but the last ones died out when the bitter cold of the last big glacier crept over the land. For close to 100,000 years no native fallow deer have lived in northern Europe or in the British Isles.

Yet fallow deer are today the most popular and widespread of all deer in Europe and Britain. They are descended from deer brought in by Phoenician and Roman traders over 2000 years ago. For centuries they were kept in vast parks and woodlands, owned by kings and noblemen, along with red deer and other animals. Some were used for "sport" but others served merely as ornaments. In 1512 one noble family had 21 parks with nearly 6000 deer in them.

Fallow deer are about the size of domestic nanny goats. They have spotted coats even when full-grown, and both sexes have a small dewlap, or flap of skin, hanging below the throat. Antlers of males are small and palmate. They sweep upward and back, and the flattened part is somewhat larger than a man's hand.

Freaks and Fawns

Mutations, or "freaks," appear in fallow deer at times, just as they do in all other animals. Nobles liked unusual things in deer so they would have something they could show off. If a fawn was born with an odd color, the nobleman who owned it would have his servants save and breed it. As a result it is now possible to find, especially in England, fallow deer that are grayish blue, brownish black, and creamy white, as well as the usual reddish color with white spots. True albinos with pink noses and eyes also crop up, but creamy white deer are not albinos, for they have dark eyes and tan-colored noses and hoofs.

Fallow deer females and their young stay together in herds but males join them only during the breeding season. Several stags usually stay with one herd. They challenge each other with a deep bellow that sounds halfway between a cough and a grunt, but when two meet they rarely fight.

Instead, they take part in a contest that is much like a ceremony. Two rivals march along, side by side, looking at each other out of the corners of their eyes. Suddenly they stop, face each other, and slam their heads together. They shove and push for a few minutes but if one does not give in they march again. Soon another clash takes place. This may happen several times before one gives a grunt and trots off.

Just before time for her fawn to be born a female leaves the herd and hunts for grass or other soft material to use for a nest. For a while she is restless, lying down for a minute, then jumping up and pacing about. When birth begins, the forefeet of the fawn appear first, with the nose and head resting on them. Soon the whole body slides out.

The newborn fawn is weak and wet, and the mother licks it thoroughly all over. This gets the young one clean and dry, and forces it to start using its muscles to move about. The licking also helps the mother and fawn to learn each other's smell. This is important for they must be able to find and recognize each other if they should become separated.

Over the centuries, fallow deer have been set free or have escaped from parks and zoos in many lands. Now half-wild or feral herds live on every continent except Antarctica. In the United States they have been seen feeding with American wild deer as well as with cattle and horses.

There is only one subspecies. Persian fallow deer are slightly larger than European ones and are extremely rare. Fewer than 100 animals live in two small patches of woodland in western Iran. Poaching is common but the main reason so few are left is that humans have taken over the places where they used to live. Wildlife parks have been set up by the government, so there is a chance the race may be saved.

India's Beautiful Deer

Chitals, or axis deer (*Axis axis*), are the most common deer of India. They are fond of water and live near rivers where both forests and dense grass thickets can be found. Adults have spotted coats and males have three-tined antlers that are cast at any time of year. These animals are slightly smaller than fallow deer and are said to be among the most beautiful of all deer.

Herds are large, usually 50 to 70 or more animals. During the rainy season, when food is plentiful, they may grow in size to one or two hundred. If food becomes scarce near the end of the dry season the herds may break up into small, widely-scattered groups. Stags go off alone only when they are growing a new set of antlers.

Chital herds often feed peacefully with other deer and even with black bucks, a kind of Indian antelope. Leaders are usually females but they change about as if taking turns. In time of danger axis deer will follow any animal that moves away steadily, whether it is a female, a male, or even a black buck.

Monkey Leftovers

Many stories are told about the curious attraction that gray langur monkeys and axis deer seem to have for each other. It is known that the deer often crowd around trees where these monkeys are feeding. Years ago it was thought the two groups might be using each other for protection. Perhaps the deer were warned of danger by monkey cries and chatter, or the langurs were alerted when frightened deer gave a bark of alarm.

The chitals are alert to danger, and will follow any other animal that is fleeing a predator. Inevitably some fail to escape.

Some naturalists who decided to keep a close watch on the two groups found out what really took place. Monkeys are messy eaters and they often take only a bite or two from a leaf or fruit before dropping it and reaching for another. The deer were simply feasting on fallen food.

One observer saw a monkey climb down a tree holding a small detached branch. A chital stag started nibbling the leaves as the monkey passed him. The monkey jerked its branch away and ran to a tall tree nearby, then scampered to the top. There it ate the leaves in peace.

Since they live in the tropics there is no rutting season for the herd as a group. A few deer of each sex are likely to be in heat during any month of the year, but a male makes no attempt to collect a company of females. Instead, he wanders from one female to another, sniffing and trying to find one that will let him court her. Few fights occur, but stags bluff each other by displaying their antlers, pawing the ground, and "preaching" on their hind legs. They chase and prance around females just as other deer do.

Newborn fawns are kept hidden for a week or more, but one naturalist was able to watch a young fawn nursing. It walked between its mother's front legs, butted her udder a couple of times, then grabbed a teat and hung on. As it sucked it held its tail high and pawed the air with one small foreleg. In less than a minute the mother walked on and the young one had to try again. Female axis deer often nurse fawns not their own.

Squatty Hog Deer

Hog deer (*Axis porcinus*) are close relatives of axis deer. They are short and squat, with coarse hair, heavy bodies, and delicate legs. These animals look even more like wild boars when they are running, for they stretch their necks, holding the head low, just as boars do when dashing from danger. Hog deer live alone except during the mating season.

Two races of hog deer are in danger of becoming extinct. Small Calamian deer in the Philippines are killed for food and Bawean deer, on an island north of Java, are being crowded out as land is taken over for agriculture. As so often happens, laws to protect these animals are not enforced.

Both species of axis deer have been introduced into other countries. In New Zealand, where no predators live, they have grown so numerous that the government hires hunters as "professional exterminators." Groups of axis deer also live in Texas, along with 34 other kinds of hoofed mammals from foreign countries, including deer, antelopes, giraffes, and wild boars.

Some of the newcomers live on ranches or in refuges, but others have escaped or been set free, and are now wild. Except for wild sheep, there are more axis deer in the United States than any other kind of foreign animal. Biologists keep a close watch to see that they do not become a threat to the well-being of native deer.

5

Antler "Wigs" and Perfume Pouches: Other Old-World Deer

Fierce little roe deer are found in forests all over Europe and much of central Asia. They are even more common than red deer, but are very different. All roe deer, for example, no matter where they live, are so much alike that they all belong to one species (*Capreolus capreolus*). Also, roe deer have never crossed a land bridge to another continent.

European roe deer are small, stumpy-tailed animals about the size of German shepherd dogs. Those in Siberia are somewhat larger. The animals live in small family groups during most of the year, but roebucks go off alone in November or December when it is time for their antlers to be shed. Around February, when the velvet is gone and the antlers are hard, they return to the does and their young.

Bucks usually come back to the same territory and the same doe. Young males are driven away, for last year's fawns are now nearly a year old, and the buck wants no rivals nearby. Young females are allowed to stay with the family group.

For about three months the family stays together. The doe then drives the roebuck away, for it is nearing time for her new fawn to be born. If twins arrive she drops them at two different places, not too close together. The fawns stay hidden for several days but the doe comes back regularly to let them nurse and to see that they are all right.

While does are busy with new fawns, roebucks wander from place to place, often going quite far. They turn homeward only when the mating season begins, toward the end of June. Some bucks go back to the same mate, but others look for a new one.

Roebucks in rut cuff the bark off trees and scrape the ground with their antlers, but do not make wallows. Each one usually chooses a piece of open ground with a rock or bush in the center, and marks it for his own. Grunting and snorting with excitement, he threshes his antlers back and forth on the rock or bush, and rubs scent on it from the glands under his eyes.

When a doe comes near an excited buck, a race is likely to begin. She may dash off through fields and woods, but usually ends up by running in circles around the bush or rock the buck has marked. At times she seems to flirt, jumping and leaping, and looking back at him. He follows behind, muzzle outstretched, sniffing, panting, and grunting. The trampled-down path that the two deer make are known as "roe rings" or "witches' circles." Finally the doe slows to a walk and lets the buck catch up with her. During the next month they may mate several times. The two stay together, in company with the fawn and female yearling, until late fall.

Young males without mates may come by and challenge the buck. If this happens, a clash is sure to follow. Roe deer fight savagely and the battle may go on until one or the other is killed. Skulls have been found with the broken tip of an antler from another buck deep inside.

Two Kinds of Development

During October and November a "false rut" takes place. For some reason not yet-known, a few does do not come in heat during the summer, but are ready to mate in the fall. These does usually pair off with young roebucks, for older ones have already taken mates.

Roe fawns are born a little over five months after the embryo starts to grow inside the mother. Yet, whether the mothers mated in the summer or in the fall, all the young are born in late spring at about the same time. How this could be was long a puzzle to deer-keepers, but scientists have now discovered that two kinds of embryo development can take place in roe deer.

Usually an embryo in any kind of animal begins to grow as soon as the sperm cell from the father unites with the egg cell of the mother. The fertilized egg then divides again and again until a very small ball of cells is formed. By this time the inside wall, or lining, of the mother's uterus has become soft and spongy, and full of blood vessels. The embryo then is "implanted" in the wall. That is, it sinks down into the layer that has been made ready for it and continues to grow.

In some kinds of animals "delayed implantation" can occur. The lining of the uterus is not prepared at the time that the egg and sperm meet, so the ball of cells goes into a resting period. It lies quietly, alive but not growing, sometimes for weeks or months. Later, when chemicals from certain glands in the mother's body act on the lining of the uterus, it is made ready for the embryo. Then the ball of cells is implanted and starts to grow again.

Delayed implantation takes place in all roe deer females that mate during the regular breeding season in the summer. In these does the ball of cells rests until the "false rut" in late fall. Then it becomes attached to the uterus wall and starts to grow. This makes it possible for all doe fawns to be born at about the same time.

Peculiar Antlers

Roebuck antlers are quite different from those of red deer and their relatives. Each roe antler is a little longer than a man's hand and it grows almost straight upward, ending in a forked tip. About halfway down is a short tine, and all the antler below it is covered with rough, knobby spurs and "stickers."

If an accident happens to an antler growing in any kind of deer, the antler probably will not be normal. Roe deer, however, seem to develop peculiar antlers more than any other species, whether or not an accident takes place. One type that is not uncommon is a very thick beam with several points growing upward from it. Sometimes growths of this sort will almost cover the whole top of the head.

In some bucks three or four separate antlers grow, each one on its own antler stalk. Other males may develop only a pair of short spikes with no branches. Bucks with antlers like this are known as "murderers" because the pointed spears can easily jab another buck and kill it.

Probably the oddest antler type is the "wig." This is a mass of antler tissue that grows until it looks like an old-fashioned straw beehive. The velvet stays on, but the mound of bone underneath becomes hard. Wigs seem to develop when something goes wrong with the chemistry of the sex organs.

Sometimes roe females develop one or two small antlers. These are never shed, and if there are two they usually do not match. Does that have antlers do not become "half-males," as some think, for such does have been seen nursing fawns. Also, several does with antlers, killed by hunters, have been found to have one or two embryos in the uterus.

Chinese Water Deer

Three subfamilies of small deer, smaller even than roe deer, live in southeastern Asia. Animals in all three groups do not look much like ordinary deer. The back is arched and the hind legs are longer than the front limbs, making the deer higher at the rump than at the shoulder. Also, all of these deer have, in the upper jaws, a pair of long tusks that have developed from the canine teeth.

Chinese water deer (*Hydropotes inermis*) are more closely related to roe deer than are either of the other two groups. The scientific name means "unarmed water-drinker" and most of these deer live in marshes along river banks in China and Korea where water is plentiful. Broad hoofs on the slender legs help the animals move freely through mud and water reeds.

Water deer are "unarmed" because they have no antlers, but their large tusks make good weapons. Each tusk is flat and swordlike, with a sharp rear edge, and is about as long as a man's thumb. When two bucks fight during the late fall breeding season they can deliver slashing cuts.

During a fight each animal tries to put his head over the other's neck. Then the tusks are used to tear out pieces of hair and skin. Most males show long scars, for the injuries are usually not serious, and soon heal.

Water deer do not form herds but live alone or in small groups of two or three animals. When danger appears they "freeze," hunched under cover until the last instant. Then they spring away in a series of leaps much as rabbits do.

Water deer were once thought to have litters of fawns, with perhaps six or seven being born at one time, but scientists now think these early reports may have been mistaken. Water deer have been kept in a number of zoos and no litters have been born there. Even the birth of triplets has been rare. In zoos, at least, and probably in the wild, water deer seem to have either one fawn or twins, just as most other kinds of deer do.

For a number of years water deer have lived in the large park at Woburn Abbey, in England, where Père David's deer were kept. These deer are so small, however, that many of them crawled through spaces in the wire fence that surrounds the park and became wild. Every few years reports come in about strange little leaping deer. Some reports add that these deer, if caught, are likely to cut deep gashes with their teeth.

Musk Deer

Musk deer, another subfamily of small deer in Asia, live high on mountains and plateaus from the Himalayas to Siberia. These are the most primitive of all deer. They are so much like their ancestors that lived millions of years ago that, for many years, some scientists thought they should not be included in the deer family. Later studies of their skeletons, stomachs, and other structures, however, showed they really were deer.

Musk deer (*Moschus moschiferus*) are stocky little animals with a small head, big ears, and a stumpy tail. Their saberlike tusks are longer than those of water deer and curve down below the jaw. Male musk deer have no antlers, and females have only two nipples instead of the usual four.

On steep snow slopes and slippery rocks, musk deer are almost as surefooted as goats. The two small hoofs on each

The male musk deer has no antlers, but has a gland, seen here beneath the body, that produces musk. This scent is very attractive to females.

foot can spread apart and grab both sides of a rough ridge. Long false claws behind the hoofs dig in for an instant and keep the animal steady as it races over uneven ground. When a musk deer is alarmed it gives a sound halfway between a hiss and a sneeze, and bounds off as if all four feet were on springs.

Even though they live in high mountain forests, musk deer have no furry undercoat. Their speckled, gray-brown fur is made of coarse hairs that are long, thin, hollow tubes. Air inside them, warmed by body heat, protects the deer during harsh winters. Travelers in Tibet often keep warm by using mattresses made of this spongy deer hair.

Musk deer live alone except during the mating season in late fall. Males in rut fight much as water deer do, ripping with their long tusks. The victor rounds up only one female but he may have to chase her for as long as 24 hours.

Precious Pouches

Musk deer are said to be the most prized catch of any wild animal in Asia. This is because males have a gland on the underside of the body, near the base of the abdomen, that produces musk. The substance is made in extra amounts during the mating season, and tempts females to come to the males.

Fresh musk has a strong, peculiar smell that seems to spread everywhere. Most persons find it disagreeable. Dried musk, however, smells pleasant and when so highly mixed with other materials that very little musk is left, it gives off an unusually sweet scent. The scientific name of these deer is well chosen, for it means "musky musk-bearers."

The gland is a skin-lined pouch about the size of a walnut. Musk freshly taken from it is soft, moist, and waxy. At first the color is yellowish-red to purple but the substance soon dries to a brownish, grainy powder. For over 3000 years it has been valued as the best base known for manufacturing long-lasting perfumes. Orientals also use musk as a love potion, or to deaden pain.

Hunters usually set snares or use traps, but sometimes they trail the deer with dogs and guns. Most of the time they take only the musk pouch, or "pod." As late as the early 1970s one pod of pure musk could be sold for what amounted to $1000 in United States money.

Around the 1940s close to 100,000 deer were killed each year. This number included many females, that have no musk, for hunters cannot tell the sex of the animal until they examine it, and snares and traps catch any kind of creature. In spite of laws to protect musk deer, poachers still kill them, smuggle out the musk pods, and get rich.

Chemists discovered how to make synthetic musk about the middle of this century. This is much less expensive, and is now used by most perfume manufacturers. Persons in the Oriental medicine trade, however, will not accept or use artificial musk, so the killing goes on.

Musk-deer farming is being tried in the Soviet republics and in China. Fresh musk can be taken from an animal by placing a hollow tube in the opening to the pouch and pressing on the gland. Musk is squirted out into a container. The deer, not hurt at all, can jump up and run out, and later produce another pouchful of the strong-scented material.

Rib-Faced Muntjacs

Animals in one subfamily of small, primitive deer have both tusks and antlers. Fossils show that muntjacs are very much like the first antlered deer that lived nearly 25 million years ago. Several species of muntjacs live in southeastern Asia and nearby Pacific islands, but probably the most common one is the muntjac of India (*Muntiacus muntjak*).

Tusks of Indian muntjacs are broader and shorter than

those of musk or water deer. Only the tips show, hanging over the lower lip. Muntjacs have soft, shiny hair, and the tongue is so long that an animal can lick clean most of its face, even the eyes.

A muntjac antler is about as long as the palm of a man's hand and it sits on a bony, fur-covered pedicel, or antler stalk, that is longer than the antler itself. The antlers are just short spikes with curved tips and a spur at the base. The two stalks continue down over the face between the eyes, and finally meet to form a V that ends at the nose.

Hunters often call muntjacs "rib-faced deer" because the bony, V-shaped ridge shows through the skin. Females also are rib-faced. They have no antlers but the top tips of the V-shaped ribs jut upward from their foreheads, forming two short stalks. Each one ends in a bony knob covered with a tuft of hair.

Muntjacs live alone or in pairs in dense forests. They eat grass and tree sprouts but also like wild fruits and fleshy flowers. Some even feed on dead animals or on eggs left in a nest on the ground. One pet muntjac became so fond of hen's eggs that he started hunting them out for himself.

Natives call muntjacs "kakurs," or barking deer, because the loud, sharp noises made by an alarmed muntjac sounds like hoarse barks. An animal may keep yelping for an hour or more until all danger is past. Very excited muntjacs make an odd clicking or rattling sound that seems to come from the throat or be produced by the teeth. One naturalist suggested jokingly that perhaps "the muntjac's teeth were chattering."

Calls during the rutting season are loud, squealing barks that are repeated over and over. These invite does to come to the male but are a warning to other bucks to keep away.

Native hunters in Borneo call the deer to them by imitating the calls on leaf whistles.

Both antlers and tusks are used when rivals fight. Muntjacs may also charge dogs or other small animals that threaten them. A cornered muntjac is likely to turn on its enemy and attack fiercely.

Chinese or Reeve's muntjacs are so small that no part of their bodies reaches higher than a human knee. Early in this century the Duke of Bedford set some free on his large estate at Woburn Abbey and hundreds of their descendants roam wild in parts of England. The animals hold a curious position, for they are now more numerous in a far-off land, where they have become feral, than in their own homeland.

The two rarest deer in the world are muntjacs. Only two Fea's muntjacs have been found, and only three black

The muntjac has a curious face formed partly of antler stalks.

muntjacs. Both have large tufts of hair on the forehead that hide the long antler stalks and part of the short antlers. Black muntjacs have such long tufts that they are called hairy-fronted muntjacs. Nothing has been heard about either of these two races for years, and they may be extinct.

The large tufts of hair on these two muntjacs help show there is a close relationship between true muntjacs and another muntjac species, the dainty tufted deer (*Elaphodus cephalophus*). These animals are not rib-faced and have short antler stalks. All but the tips of the daggerlike antlers are hidden by blackish hair on the forehead, which grows in a sort of horseshoe-shaped crest. The scientific name, which means "deer with a head-crest," was chosen because of this tuft.

Muntjac Records

Indian muntjacs have been used in studies of sleep patterns. Scientists report that these animals appear to sleep for only about 25 seconds at a time, which seems to be a record for mammals. Muntjacs are almost constantly on the alert, searching for food, watching over their young, or on the lookout for enemies such as leopards, tigers, wolves, or eagles.

Indian muntjacs hold another record. They have the lowest number of chromosomes of any mammal yet studied. Chromosomes are very minute structures in the cells of our bodies that control all that we inherit from our parents, such as how tall we grow or what color eyes and hair we have.

Human beings have 46 chromosomes in each cell. Most deer have 56 to 70 chromosomes, but male Indian muntjacs have only seven chromosomes, and the females have six. Their closest relative, the Reeve's muntjac, has 46.

6

The Mighty Moose-Elk

American moose, which are exactly the same species as the European elk (*Alces alces*), are the biggest and in a way the most magnificent of all deer, yet at the same time the most awkward and ugliest. Their humped shoulders are nearly as high as the top of an ordinary door, and the stiltlike legs are so long the animals can walk through hip-high snow or step over fallen trees. Wide-splayed hoofs let them wade through squelchy bogs where nearly any other animal would sink to its death.

The moose's long face is topped by two donkeylike ears and ends in a wide, squared-off muzzle that hangs over the lower lip. This droopy snout is useful for breaking branches or stripping leaves from trees, but Pliny the Elder, a Roman naturalist who lived nearly 2000 years ago, thought it got in the animal's way. He wrote that elk had to go backward when they grazed, for if they went forward the large upper lip would get doubled up on itself.

Instead of growing upward as those of other deer do, moose antlers stick out sideways from the roof of the skull. They are palmate with huge, flattened plates sometimes armed with 40 or more tines. A short, thick neck supports this heavy weight.

Both sexes have a hairy flap of skin, called a dewlap, or bell, that hangs under the throat. In males it is usually about as long as the distance from an adult human's elbow to his wrist, but bulls in their prime sometimes have one as

The hairy skin flap beneath an adult moose's neck has no function that zoologists know of. Perhaps it was once useful but may be now gradually disappearing in the course of evolution.

long as a human arm. No one has yet discovered a use for the dangling strip.

True elk live in northern forests in lands all around the north pole. Their favorite haunts are marshy woods with plenty of willow and poplar trees. An elk standing on its hind legs can reach up and pull down branches nearly twice as high as it is.

To reach leaves still higher a moose will straddle a young tree, often as big around as a man's leg, and push it

A moose has an ingenious method of getting the most bark possible from a young, flexible tree.

over. Then it "rides" it down to the end, eating as it goes. The heavy body is likely to cause the tree trunk to snap in two. Because the animal is so fond of tender twigs, Indians called it a "moose," which means "twig-eater," and early American pioneers adopted the name.

It is impossible for long-legged, short-necked moose to munch ground plants or drink water while standing. An animal must either spread its front legs widely as giraffes do or get down on its knees. In spring, when new shoots begin to show, a moose can often be seen hunching along on its knees, cropping tender sprouts.

Moose usually wade into water to drink, and to eat a favorite food, water lilies. They even dive deeply to tug loose crisp and juicy stalks. The big rump with its finger-length tail usually comes up first, half the time turned awkwardly sideways. Then the moose's head appears, streaming water and with long shreds of moss and pondweeds hanging from its mouth and antlers.

Moose also like odd foods. Lee Crandall, former director of the Bronx Zoo in New York City, said moose there were fond of bananas. Randolph Peterson, in his book on North American moose, told of a partly tamed one that liked chewing-tobacco so well it would nudge visitors, begging for some. If no tobacco was given him he was likely to butt the person who refused.

The Largest Living Deer

Elk have lived in northern forests of Europe and Asia for hundreds of thousands of years. Primitive men hunted them and left charred elk bones by their campfires. Pictures of ancient European elk painted on cave walls have been discovered in southern Europe.

Elk from Asia made the long trip to North America by way of Beringia about the same time as wapitis. When glaciers melted back, the elk spread south and east. Shifting ice sheets and open grasslands divided them into groups that remained separate for thousands of years. As a result, four races developed.

The largest of the four is the Alaskan moose (*Alces alces gigas*). These animals are the size of the long-dead giant deer of Europe, although their huge antlers do not spread nearly as wide. Moose are so powerful they seem not to be afraid either of animals such as bears or packs of wolves or of any machines.

Even jet planes do not frighten the creatures. A 1962 news report told of a bull moose that wandered onto an airfield at Anchorage, Alaska, and became bothered by a noisy jet getting ready for a take-off. He attacked it head first, and when the noise had stopped enough to suit him he trotted off into the forest. The plane was not damaged enough to delay the flight very long, but mechanics had to make a safety check.

Although they can travel in fairly deep snow, moose like to stroll down snow-cleared highways and railroad tracks, and expect to have the right-of-way. Northern trains have often been late because a moose had to be nudged out of the way. If a speeding locomotive should slam into a moose the blow could shove some cars off the track as well as kill the moose.

Car drivers in northern lands also need to watch out for the big animals. If a moose sees a huge, noisy monster rushing down on him, his first action is to defend himself. Using his great weight and sharp hoofs a moose can easily smash and wreck a car. A driver is lucky who is only left stranded, not hurt.

Ancient Elk

Moose have no living close relatives, but they do have some interesting extinct ones. Fossils of two early elk in Europe show how the wide, flattened antlers probably developed. Gallic elk, which lived over a million years ago, had antlers with enormously long beams that stuck out sideways. At the end of each was a small, upturned saucer with a few tines around the rim. The whole antler looked like a long-handled spoon.

Broad-fronted elk followed them half a million years later. In these animals the flattened plate was much larger and took up about half the length of the beam. Another quarter of a million years passed before elk antlers developed the oversized plates that are familiar to us today.

Fossils of another kind of ancient elk have been discovered in America. Cervalces, the great stag-moose, had large antlers with only small plates, but on the underside of each beam was a piece of bone formed into a trumpet shape. Skulls of these animals were unusually thick and heavy. Stag-moose fossils have been found from Alaska to New Jersey and as far south as Oklahoma. A skeleton of one is now in the Princeton Museum.

Mating Moose

Elk or moose do not live in herds. Normally peaceful, even shy, each one lives alone. In midwinter when several may be forced to "yard" near one another for a few days, each keeps to himself as much as possible. The "yard" is just a close network of trails and moose are together only because food is there.

When the mating season begins in September, males become short-tempered and are ready to attack any creature they think might be a rival. Bulls hunting for females crash through the forest, often gouging the bark off trees and trampling anything in their paths. Sometimes one paws a pit in the ground, urinates in it, then wallows in the mud. The mating call may be anything from a low bellow to a deep, muffled roar.

Females invite bulls to come to them with a hoarse bleat or bawl that ends in a coughing grunt. When the two meet, the bull does not drive the cow to some place of his choosing, as many deer do. She goes where she pleases and he follows. Usually a bull stays with one cow for a week or ten days until she is ready to accept him. He mates with her several times, then leaves to seek another partner.

Real fights are rare. When two bulls meet, a lot of grunting and antler thrashing is likely to take place, ending with a little sparring. This is chiefly a shoving match and lets the bulls see which one is stronger.

If a fight does develop it is violent. The two bang and slash at each other, ripping branches from nearby trees as they push and struggle. Finally, with skin torn and bleeding, the weaker one gives in and runs away. By mid-November the rut is over.

Clumsy Calves

Calves, often twins, are born in May or June. Just before they arrive, the yearling, awkward and frightened, is run off and the cow hunts for a safe, lonely thicket. The newborn calf has no spots and its legs seem to be twice too long for its gangly body.

At first the cow may kneel or lie down for the wobbly calf to nurse, but this is not needed for long. Calves double their weights within three weeks. Moose infants are said to grow faster than the young of any other wild mammal in North America.

Mothers with young calves are as quick to fight as bulls are during the rutting season. Until the young one is able to escape on its own she will attack with her sharp hoofs any creature that comes close enough to be a threat. One moose mother was seen to drive off two husky dogs. Another chased a good-sized bear up a tree and kept it there until she and her calf finished feeding.

Tamed Moose

Moose are easily tamed and males do not become vicious when full-grown as do roe deer and red deer. Northern trappers and farmers say that moose make good pets, but few bother to tame them. It is a different story in Russia and the Baltic countries where smaller European elk live. Many people have bottle-raised these moose from infancy, and a few have trained them to work.

The young are captured when they are from one to three days old and are fed cow's milk. Dr. Lutz Heck, a retired professor in Berlin, Germany, tells of a forester who had a pet male moose that learned to jump into and out of the house through an open window. It roamed freely about, upstairs and down, but stayed in the living room during meals. Out in the forest it followed its owner as would a dog. It could be ridden bareback, but would have nothing to do with a saddle.

Young ones can be trained to walk on a leash when

three or four months old. Moose follow their keeper readily, but teaching them to pull a heavy load to a certain place, with the keeper behind them, may take up to two or three years. A full-grown moose can carry on its back a load equal to one-third its weight, and harnessed to a sleigh it can pull a load equal to its weight. Since moose need neither stables nor special food they may turn out someday to be of much use in northern Siberia.

Ups and Downs

Moose have been important to northern American Indians for thousands of years. Trappers and early settlers in North America learned to depend on moose, too, and soon the great animals were overhunted. By the beginning of the nineteenth century great areas of forest land in central and eastern North America had no moose at all.

During the twentieth century moose populations have been slowly growing again. About 12,000 of the animals now live in the lower 48 states with perhaps 120,000 in Alaska. In the few western states where moose are found, a certain quota can be taken by hunters each year.

Poaching is common, however, and the illegal kill is often almost double the quota. In one county in Idaho, for example, during the 1973-74 season, the quota was 40, but the total number killed was around 100. Little or nothing is done about the problem. If overkill continues, moose will stand a chance of being wiped out in these sections.

In a few areas, such as parts of Maine, there are too many moose for the amount of land set aside for them. Wolves, the main predators of moose, were driven from this region long ago. No hunting seasons have been allowed since 1934. Under conditions such as these, when not enough predators are present to keep the animals healthy by culling the misfits, and much food is at hand, overpopulation is likely to follow.

When many animals are crowded together, this usually brings on a high number of deaths. If food runs out some will starve. Others become weak and ill. Infectious diseases spread easily.

Moose Disease

Moose in overcrowded areas, where white-tailed deer are also common, often fall prey to a disease known as "moose sickness." An infected animal becomes weak, loses control of its movements and stumbles aimlessly about. Often it wanders in circles, holding its head in an odd position on one side or the other. Some moose go blind. Finally the legs become paralyzed. No longer able to take care of itself, the animal dies.

Moose disease is caused by a small, threadlike worm that lives a part of its life in snails or slugs. Grazing animals may swallow the small, infected creatures along with their food. Minute young worms, called larvae, are set free and begin to travel through the animal's body. They move along the nerves, get into the spinal cord, and finally reach the brain.

These microscopic brain worms are quite common in white-tailed deer, but do not seem to cause much trouble there. Adult worms mate, and worm eggs are passed out with waste from the deer's intestines. Wherever deer graze, snails and slugs are likely to become infected.

Moose become victims of this disease when too many moose and too many deer are crowded together in the same area. Since deer carry the disease, the chances are high that the overcrowded moose will sooner or later swallow infected snails or slugs. No cure for the disease is known, and there is no way to get rid of the hundreds of thousands of snails and slugs that live in forests. The only sure control is to find some means of cutting down the deer population.

Paradise in Lake Superior

Moose have played an important part in one of the most unusual studies wildlife biologists have been able to carry out. The experiment really began early in this century on a long, narrow island in Lake Superior, about 24 kilometers (about 15 miles) from Canada's border. Isle Royale was then a paradise for any large, browsing animal.

A few moose found it about 1912. Probably they swam to the island, for moose are good swimmers. With no enemies and plenty of food the number of moose shot up each year. Before the 1920s ended, close to 3000 hungry moose were stripping bark from trees and eating young shoots so fast there was no chance for more to grow. Starvation and disease spread, and hundreds died.

After several years of drought, followed by a big wilderness fire in 1936, many people thought moose were gone from the island for good. But rains came again, young trees grew, and back came the moose. This time there was a difference. A breeding pack of wolves appeared in the late 1940s. Probably they had traveled from Canada over frozen lake ice.

Wildlife biologists realized that Isle Royale, now a National Park, was a dream come true. An outdoor laboratory waited for them there with a population of the world's biggest antlered animal, together with that animal's natural predator, the wolf. Now they could learn, without interference, just what free-roaming wolves would do to moose. In the long run would the wolves help or harm the great animals?

The Isle Royale Study

Dr. Durward L. Allen, wildlife professor at Purdue University, in Indiana, and some of his graduate students set up a ten-year study. They learned that during the winter the wolf pack killed and ate a moose every three or four days. A healthy moose was rarely harmed, for when an attack came it laid back its ears, lashed out with its forefeet, and almost dared the wolves to come closer. A weak or injured moose that tried to run away was nearly always killed and eaten.

Wolves stalk and "test" about 12 moose for every one they kill. They are able to take only the very young or very old, or the weak, the sick, or the injured. In most cases these are the ones that need to be culled and destroyed anyway, if the moose population is to remain healthy.

After a few years moose and wolves on Isle Royale reached an almost steady balance. The number of moose killed each year just about matched the number of young ones that were born and able to live through their first year. Also, the moose were in good condition. Without any doubt they had been helped by the wolves, not harmed by them.

As time goes on trees on the island will grow old, and too big and tall for the moose to use. New young trees will be needed, but they do not grow well in the shade of the old. Chances are good, however, that another lightning-caused fire will open up the forest and start the cycle all over again. What we see as disasters, such as forest fires, are often a necessary part of balance in nature.

7

Deer of the Freezing Far North

Reindeer are remarkable animals. They live farther north than any other deer and can stand more cold. They live in larger herds and migrate longer distances. Females wear antlers, and shed them each year just as males do, although at a different time. Also, reindeer are the only members of the deer family that have ever been domesticated and used in human service for thousands of years.

Much of a reindeer's life is spent on the tundra. This is a wide belt of land just south of the Arctic Ocean where winters are long and dark, and frost can occur at any time of the year. During the short, cool summers only the topsoil thaws. Then the flat land becomes a great, chilly swamp, because the meltwater cannot drain away through the frozen ground below. Low ground plants grow here, and a few dwarfed trees and shrubs.

Reindeer are well suited for life in this land. Their thick, shaggy fur is made of hollow hairs that hold in body heat particularly well and help the animal stay afloat when it swims across an icy stream. Even the ears and nose are furred, except for a small, bare spot on the tip of the snout.

The two broad hoofs on each foot spread widely and keep the animal from sinking when it walks on snow or marshy ground. Back of the hoofs are long, heavy false claws that reach to the ground and help support the weight. In winter the hoofs grow longer and the pads beneath the foot shrink and become horny, leaving hard, half-moon-shaped rims. These provide traction, just as studded tires do, and make it easier for deer to walk on ice and frozen snow.

Frozen Food

Reindeer eat grass, sedges, and other plants, but the favorite food is "reindeer moss," a kind of bushy lichen. These plants grow in thick tufts all over the tundra as well as in the evergreen forests where reindeer spend the winter. Freezing does not harm lichens. If they are covered by snow the deer paw it away. Reindeer also chew on cast antlers, probably for the minerals they contain.

Some of the eating habits are peculiar. At times deer feed on little ratlike animals called lemmings, that are stamped to death with the forefeet. Fish, and dead animals left where deer can reach them, are also devoured. Reindeer are fond of puffballs and mushrooms, and eat all kinds, even the poisonous ones. These seem not to hurt the animals, but only to make them sleepy and slow, and more easily captured. Reindeer are also greedy for salt and will eat seaweed, drink sea water, and lick up urine.

Reindeer Servants

Most northern tribes in Europe and Asia have made use of reindeer for as long as anyone can remember. Probably a number of tribes domesticated various groups of the animals at different times. From evidence that scientists have dug up we know that reindeer had been put into service in central Siberia as long as 3000 years ago. Dogs may have been used in rounding up the animals, for they were domesticated thousands of years before that time. Reindeer herders today say that ten dogs are worth 20 men when they want to head the animals off or make them go in another direction.

At first deer may have been penned up for a while by being stampeded into some dead-end canyon or staked-off artificial trap. Having a few animals close at hand when meat or hides were needed was much better than having to go on a long hunt. Later the hunters may have realized they could keep deer penned for a longer period, especially in winters, if the place where they were held was large enough for the animals to find plenty to eat.

Learning to gain control over reindeer herds is very different from domesticating other useful animals such as cattle, goats, and horses, because reindeer go on long migrations twice a year. In the spring they journey northward, sometimes for great distances, to reach their summer feeding grounds. After weeks of feeding and resting, reindeer follow the same paths south again when freezing temperatures return and snowstorms start.

Herders could do nothing to stop the migrations. Deer had to find their own food, and this was the way they did it. Families who wanted to keep reindeer had to be nomads. They followed their own small herds north in the spring, and south again in the fall. Also, they had to find some way to keep their animals from joining wild herds. Perhaps they used dogs, or tempted the animals with salty bait foods.

Finally reindeer became used to humans' ways. They seemed content to work for them as long as they could follow that deep urge within and migrate twice a year. After domestication took place, living animals could be used, as well as dead ones. Some deer were taught to carry a man on their backs. Others were trained to wear a harness and pull a sleigh.

Females were milked, but each time they had to be caught and led away from the herd. No reindeer is content to stay alone. Today reindeer cows are lassoed by their antlers, which then have to be held or tied tightly. Otherwise a sudden swipe of the reindeer's head might injure the milker badly. Sometimes, if it is time for antlers to be shed, a lassoed cow runs off, leaving her antlers behind. Then she has to be lassoed by the neck or another cow caught.

Lapland

Most people in Europe today who depend on reindeer for a living are found in Lapland. This is not a country in itself but a region that stretches across four countries in the most northern part of Europe: Norway, Sweden, Finland, and the Soviet Union. Lapps are a minority, for the total in all four countries together is only about 35,000 to 40,000. In some ways Lapps are like our own American Indians, for they have their own language and customs. In recent years, however, many have given up the old ways of life.

Less than a third of the Lapps still herd reindeer, but these few depend almost entirely on the animals for all their needs. Milk, cheese, and reindeer meat are their most basic foods. Skins are used for tents, clothing, and bedding. When cash is needed for such things as coffee, salt, or something made of metal such as a knife blade, a reindeer is caught and sold.

Some herdsmen today live in settled homes. They turn the deer loose in May to make the long migrations alone, then round them up in the fall when they return. Each person can tell his own animal by marks cut into the ear.

Other deer herders are still nomads, and they make the

Meat, milk, and skin are provided for Laplanders by reindeer, and the animals are additionally useful for pulling sleds.

long trips with their reindeer. Families live in deerskin tents on these journeys, and carry all their belongings with them on canoe-shaped sleds pulled by reindeer. The trip each way takes about a month.

Most domesticated herds range in size from about 100 to 1000. Calves are born during the spring migration, and rut occurs on the return trip in the fall. Herders allow only a few of the young males to mate. They cut the testicles off the other male deer so that the animals cannot produce sperm. After this operation the males do not come into rut, and remain gentle.

New Ways of Life

Today herd management is changing. Some owners use motor sleds to round up and drive the deer. Instead of following the migrating herds on sleds, women and children often make the long trip in trucks, and join the men and deer at journey's end. About 1967 a number of herdsmen began trucking their entire herds from winter to summer ranges and back again. One reason, they said, was that grazing along the routes had become so poor the animals could not find enough food along the way.

Reindeer land itself is changing. Cities are being built, rivers dammed for hydroelectric plants, and mines opened up. Highways and railroads that are needed to carry supplies cut across migration routes. Forests are clear-cut, then replanted with fast-growing trees for the lumber industry. This destroys the lichens, and it takes half a century for these plants to grow large enough again to be useful.

If traffic is not too great, deer will cross highways or railroad tracks, and each year hundreds of them are killed. In some places fences have been built to funnel deer beneath bridges or across highways at certain spots, but these have been helpful only where deer could follow their normal patterns of movement. Hydroelectric plants have been even more troublesome, for dams in some places have caused both rangelands and migration routes to become flooded.

Reindeer are frightened by unfamiliar noises. Using snowmobiles for herding seems to be helpful, but sometimes they cause panic among pregnant cows, and calves are lost. Also, the price of the machines and of the gas needed to run them is often too much for herders who have only reindeer to furnish cash.

No one yet knows just what the longtime effect will be on herds that have been taken from one range to another by truck. When they are broken up into small groups for such travel, reindeer seem not to be able to form proper herds again when the animals are put together. With no means of following their urge to migrate over centuries-old trails they seem to become confused, and mill around restlessly.

Many of the animals scatter. Others seem to be at a complete loss as to what to do or where to go. It is possible the young ones may be the most affected by truck travel, for they never have a chance to learn the migration routes.

Too little is known about reindeer behavior to make any predictions about what will finally happen. Perhaps reindeer will become adjusted to modern ways of life and machines. It is also possible that migratory behavior in these herds may forever be lost. No one knows just how necessary migration is to reindeer herds if they are to stay healthy and normal.

North American Reindeer

Three kinds of deer made the long trip from Asia into North America by way of Beringia during the Ice Age. Red deer came first, and later became known as American elk, or wapiti. Not long afterwards European elk followed this northern route to a new world, and were called moose by early settlers. Still later, reindeer migrated to this continent and they, also, have been given a new name. American reindeer, known as caribou, and Old World reindeer are two races of the same species, *Rangifer tarandus*.

Although caribou were never domesticated, they have

been the mainstay of Eskimos and northern Indians for thousands of years. For traders, explorers, missionaries, and early settlers the animals were a steady source of food. Today many northern tribes still depend almost completely on caribou for food, clothing, shelter, weapons, and tools. Even the fat is burned for heat and light. The lives and customs of the people are closely bound to caribou.

Old World reindeer are about the size of white-tailed deer, but caribou are as tall as wapitis and nearly as heavy. The antlers are quite different from those of any other deer. Even on the same animal the two antlers are not alike. The big main beam is flattened rather than rounded. It slants backward and to the side, then arches upward and forward, ending in a small, flat palm. Tines branch out at odd angles.

Most peculiar are the brow tines. They grow down over the face, and one of the two, especially in caribou, reaches almost to the nose. It is spread out in a flat plate at the end and was once called the "snow shovel" because the animals were thought to use it to flip snow away from lichens. Antlers of females are much smaller than those of males, and the brow tines may be either small knobs or short shovels. Young deer only a few months old have spike antlers as long as a man's hand.

Caribou can be divided into two big groups. Woodland caribou are large, dark animals that live in the evergreen forests that spread across North America. Although once common in our border states, few are now found south of Canada except for mountain caribou, a western race of this group. Mountain caribou range at times into northern Idaho, but they are rarely sighted in other states.

A migration of barren-ground caribou is an impressive sight as they stream northward each spring by the thousands.

Great Migrations

Barren-ground caribou, the second group, are somewhat smaller than woodland caribou, and have paler coats. A long mane hangs on the underside of the throat, and both it and the neck are creamy white. Like reindeer, barren-ground caribou migrate northward to the tundra each spring. In autumn, when storms begin, they go south again to the shelter of spruce and fir forests.

Barren-ground caribou form immense herds. During winter the great groups are somewhat broken up as the animals roam through the forest looking for food, but in March, when the northward migration begins, herds form again. By dozens, then by hundreds and thousands, caribou stream northward in long, straggling lines. Year after year they follow the same trails until the paths are sometimes so deeply cut that they still show a century later.

Bands of pregnant cows come first. The animals usually look motheaten and skinny, for they are shedding their

heavy coats and winter diets are not fattening. Caribou eat on the move, a bite here and another there. It takes a month or two to reach the high protected areas which are the herd's calving grounds. The cows hurry to reach there before birth takes place.

Calves are dropped among melting snowdrifts in **May** or early June. Twenty-four hours later the calf can outrun a man on the springy tundra, and by the second day it can keep up with its mother. Within four weeks antler spikes start to grow.

Females lose their antlers about the time the young are born. Antler knobs soon show again, and growth continues during the summer months. The velvet is usually shed in late October soon after rut begins.

Females that are not carrying calves make the spring migration with the bulls. They start northward not long after the pregnant cows leave. These animals are not pressed for time and go more slowly than the cows but, like all caribou, they eat on the move. The bulls join the early group of females near the calving grounds, and by July the herd is together again.

Caribou spend most of the summer feeding on the rich plant life that covers the valleys. They are bothered by insects, especially on windless days, for swarms of small biting creatures swoop down on them by the hundreds of thousands. The tormented deer sometimes run around in panic trying to escape.

Some of them try to find higher ground. Others hunt for streams or snowbanks where they can wallow in the cool wetness. Antlers of bucks are in full velvet now and are very sensitive. The big bulls shake their heads savagely at times, trying to rid themselves of the pesky biters.

South to Winter Homes

The first frosts come in August. Most of the flies, mosquitoes, and gnats now disappear, and the animals scatter widely. For a month they eat, rest, and build up their strength as they drift slowly southward.

Rut takes place in October and early November, about the time the herds reach the treeline. Antlers are hard and clean now, and bulls are full of bluster. Woodland caribou males collect groups of ten to 15 females during the mating season, but tundra bucks spend no time rounding up cows. They rush about through the herd panting, bellowing, and courting one female after another.

By the end of the rut the herds are in full migration southward, with bulls in the lead. Winter quarters are usually reached early in December. Old males begin to drop their antlers soon after rut is over, but some of the younger bucks may keep theirs as late as February. In March velvet knobs appear on all the males.

"Buffalo of the North"

Caribou are sometimes called the "buffalo of the North" because there are such enormous herds and they range over so much territory. In the middle 1800s millions of shaggy bison, or buffaloes, thundered across our western plains, but with the coming of railroads, traders, settlers, and "gold fever," they all but disappeared. By 1900 only 800 were left. Today there is one small wild herd in Yellowstone National Park, and a few captive herds are scattered here and there.

Caribou are beginning to go the same way. In 1968 over a million American reindeer roamed the Alaskan wilderness, but just ten years later, in 1978, the number had dwindled to 400,000. The migration of a great herd of thousands of animals is said to be one of the most awe-inspiring sights in nature. If migrations are ever interfered with so greatly that the herds become confused and broken up, there is little chance the damage will ever be undone.

Because they are wilder than other reindeer, caribou seem to be even more disturbed by sights and sounds that do not belong to the wilderness. Not only pipelines, but road construction, low-flying aircraft, snowmobiles, blasting, and the noises and activity of people and machinery all tend to "spook" the animals. Some oil company ecologists say that oil fields and caribou mix quite well, because they have seen caribou crawl under elevated pipelines, and noted that some use the graded crossings made for them. But this is only part of the story.

Caribou and the Energy Crunch

Wildlife researchers have recently made a study of the behavior of caribou that came across such a pipeline. Of 6000 animals studied they found that a little over one-fifth either crawled under the structure or crossed over the gravel ramp and got to the other side. Slightly over two-fifths trotted along beside it, trying to find a way to go around. The other caribou, a little less than half the group, turned back and did not try to get past the strange object.

Other studies have shown that some herds seem to split into two parts, with a group on each side of the pipeline. However, it is the bolder bulls that usually make the crossing. Cows and calves are much less likely to do so. If one of the herds divided in this way should end up with only a few cows and calves, the unbalance might well cause it to die out in a few years' time.

Although no one yet knows what will finally happen to caribou, one recent decision of the government promises to be more of a help than a hindrance. The approved route for the new gas pipeline will not cut through the caribou calving grounds along the Arctic coast, as many had feared it might, or open a path through their winter quarters. Instead the route is to go through territory that is already disturbed. It will parallel the oil pipeline halfway through Alaska, then turn at Fairbanks and follow the Alaskan highway for some distance before it angles south.

Without doubt we need oil and gas and other forms of energy, but many people question our right to use up in one or two centuries the resources that it has taken natural forces hundreds of thousands of years to make and store. What will happen then? The whole problem is far larger than just caribou and pipelines.

We *can* get along without caribou, even though they are beautiful and awe-inspiring, and extremely important to many northern people. We can also get along without oil and gas. People did do without these forms of energy for most of the time that human beings have lived on earth. But we cannot develop—or perhaps even stay alive—without a balance among living things.

We know very little about nature's systems of checks and balances, and understand even less. Instead of rushing in to change nature, as we so often do, we might be better off to go slowly and save as much of our natural world as possible, at least until we understand better just what we are doing.

8

Pigmies, Whitetails, and Other New-World Deer

American deer have an unusual history. The small spike-antlered and branch-antlered deer of South America, as well as the more northern whitetails and mule deer, have no relatives in Europe or Asia. None of them crossed Beringia during the Ice Age as did our "adopted" deer, the wapiti, moose, and caribou. American deer developed in the Americas.

Strange little semi-deer lived in Eurasia millions of years ago. They are known as paleomerycids or "ancient cud-chewers," and were probably the ancestors of both giraffes and modern deer. Fossils of these animals, 30 million years old, have been found not only in Asia and Europe, but also in North America. These animals reached the New World, coming across Beringia, millions of years before the Ice Age began.

One of these ancient creatures was a slim-legged little animal now known as Blastomeryx, a name that means "budding cud-chewer." It was not as large as a good-sized dog, and had canine tusks, but no antlers, much as musk deer do today. Blastomeryx lived for close to 20 million years, for the species did not die out until about five million years ago.

Another ancient semi-deer, Dromomeryx, or "running cud-chewer," lived in North America from about 18 to 12 million years ago. It had short antlers on long, bony pedicels, much like those of today's muntjacs. One of its relatives had

The shy pudus, smallest of the deer, live in mountainside forests. Their size led in one case to their being used as city pets by apartment-dwellers.

a third horn in the middle of its head.

We do not know which of the ancient deerlike animals was the ancestor of modern American deer. Some fossils of early ones have been found. A few are up to about 15 million years old, but most are younger. We will have to wait for more discoveries before we can know the full history of deer in the New World.

The World's Smallest Deer

The most primitive American deer live in South America. One of these, the pigmy or dwarf deer (*Pudu pudu*), is the smallest deer in the world. Males are about the size of Irish terriers, and females are even smaller. Adult pigmies have short ears and small spike antlers that are almost hidden in the thick fur of their rounded heads.

Chilean pudus live in mountain forests as far south as the tip of South America. Another species lives near the equator, but still in mountainside forests. The animals are shy and rarely seen, but natives chase them with dogs and kill many.

If adults are captured they fight for freedom, often until they die of exhaustion. Young pudus, however, are easily tamed. Ivan Sanderson, a naturalist, told of pudus raised in an apartment in Paris, France, and treated as dogs. People who saw them being walked on the streets usually thought they were ordinary pets.

Spike-Antlered Brockets

South American deer known as brockets form another group of primitive deer with short, unbranched antlers. The term "brocket" was once used in Europe for red deer bucks in their second year. Several species of these small animals live in the northern two-thirds of the continent.

Red brockets (*Mazama americana*) are the largest of the group and probably best known. They are no larger than roe deer, and are found from Amazon River jungles north into Mexico. Brockets have arched backs and high hindquarters, and their spike antlers are a little longer than an average man's middle finger. The face has an odd look because the hair radiates out in all directions from two whorls, one on top of the head and the other below and in front of the eyes.

Brockets usually live alone. They hide during the day

but at night come to the forest edge to feed. Melons, cabbages, and other garden crops are favorite foods and angry farmers often chase them with dogs. Unlike many deer, brockets cannot run swiftly. Sometimes one is killed and eaten by the dogs before the hunter catches up with them.

Largest Deer of South America

Three groups of South American deer have branched antlers. Marsh deer (*Blastocerus dichotomus*), the largest of these, are somewhat taller and heavier than North American white-tailed deer. The scientific name means "a budding horn that forks." These animals usually live in small family groups made up of a male, one or two females, and their fawns.

Marsh deer like best the swampy areas along the banks of creeks and rivers south of the Amazon jungles. When they walk, the big hoofs spread widely apart and a membrane between the toes helps keep them from sinking. Long, heavy false claws on each foot also help support the weight.

The antlers of these deer are forked, sometimes two or three times, and the ears are quite large. Although the meat is poor and not often eaten, the animals are commonly hunted. The skins bring in a little money, and the antlers are ground up and made into love potions or medicine. Such medicine is said to help pregnant women give birth more easily.

Endangered Pampas Deer

Pampas deer (*Ozotoceros bezoarticus*) are slender, long-legged, speedy animals about two-thirds as tall as marsh deer.

They live on the dry, open grasslands of central and southern South America. An odd feature of these animals is a strong garlic scent that is given off from glands between the toes. The smell is especially strong and unpleasant in males during rut, or when the animals are suddenly roused from rest.

During most of the year these deer live in pairs or in small family groups. If danger threatens, a mother will stand guard while her fawn runs to hide. Unlike most does, she sometimes gives the young one time to escape while she draws attention to herself by limping or pretending to be hurt. Then she races off in a direction opposite to the way the fawn went.

Pampas deer are the most endangered deer of South America. So much of the grassland they depend on has been taken up by farms and ranches that the animals have little land left for them. In addition, many have died of foot-and-mouth disease and other infections brought in by cattle. Ranchmen offer no help for they hate the odor of the deer and want to get rid of the animals.

Goatlike Deer

Guemals, or south Andean deer (*Hippocamelus bisulcus*), are short-legged, stout-bodied animals a little taller than pampas deer. They live in high ranges of the Andes mountains and are very sure-footed in climbing about over the craggy or forested slopes. South America has no native goats and these deer, more than any other animal, seem to take their place.

Both male and female guemals have small upper canine teeth, but the tusks are not as long as those of water deer. The ears are quite large, the antlers forked, and a Y-shaped black streak runs down the face. The scientific name of these mountain deer has been changed at least 21 times, for no one could decide just what they were. (Such name changes occur for certain animals—and plants—more often than many people realize.) The name they now have describes the antlers, but not the animal. It means "horse-camel with two-pronged antlers."

Another species of Andean deer lives in the more northern regions of the Andes. Both are endangered and have become quite rare in some areas because red, fallow, and axis deer, brought in as game animals, have almost driven these and other native deer to extinction. Not much has been done to correct this, yet the Chileans honor the guemal. Along with the condor it is featured on the Chilean coat of arms.

American Whitetails

White-tailed deer (*Odocoileus virginianus*) are the best known of all American deer. Half a dozen races are found in the more northern countries of South America. Others live in Central America and in Mexico. Another two dozen races are scattered over North America. Except for a few areas in the Far West they are found all across the continent and up to the northern edge of the pine forests in Canada.

Although the muzzles, chins, and underparts of these deer are white, it is the whiteness of the feathery tail that holds the attention. Reddish-brown on top and white below, the tail is often all one sees as a startled animal bounds away. When it is held high in the air, the long, white hairs on its underside spread out to form a shining signal.

A deer that wants to sneak away from danger will

clamp its tail against its rear so that little or no white shows. If suddenly flipped up, the white flag is a signal of alarm to all deer nearby. During courtship the tail wags and waves violently.

Those who want to creep close to photograph deer say that the tail must be watched carefully. A quick tail-twitch in a feeding deer is a sign the deer is about to raise its head and look around. It can see the slightest motion, even a moving eyelid. The watcher must freeze instantly or the deer is likely to bound away in long, graceful leaps, tail stiffly upright.

Whitetails have been clocked at speeds of 40 kilometers (nearly 25 miles) an hour, but one in a hurry can go a third again as fast. Without a running start one can sail over a fence higher than the ceiling of an ordinary room, although most deer will try to go through or around a fence if that is possible. Both whitetails and mule deer can easily clear a car or leap across a two-lane highway without touching the pavement.

It is the whitetail that Americans usually have in mind when they use the word "deer" (whether they realize it or not); in Europe it refers to the roe deer. However, all sorts of confusions have arisen in popular images of "a deer," as on Christmas cards, decorations, and in depictions of "Rudolph." Various antlers are shown on bodies of whitetails, such as those of wapitis or of mule deer; and many are simply imaginary antlers.

Antlers and Hormones

Antlers of whitetails are quite different from those of any other deer. Each one grows backward for a short distance, giving off a small spike, then curves outward and forward to form a large half-circle held high above the head. One to four short, unbranched tines grow along its length, each pointing upward.

Scientists studying antler growth in whitetails have discovered that the whole process is controlled by three glands in the body which make special chemicals called hormones. The pituitary gland, which is not much larger than a cherry, is on the underside of the brain. One of its hormones is carried by the bloodstream to the testes. These are the male sex organs that produce sperm cells. They also manufacture the male sex hormone, called testosterone.

In the spring, when days grow longer, the eye nerves are stimulated by extra light. This causes them to activate the cherry-sized gland, and it produces more hormone. Influenced by this chemical, the testes then begin to make more testosterone, and antler growth begins. How fast antlers grow is controlled by the thyroid gland in the neck. Antlers are shed in midwinter when testosterone production slows down.

Normal males also produce a small amount of estrogen, the female sex hormone. If a large dose of estrogen is given to a male deer, this will keep the pituitary gland from sending out its hormone. Then antlers do not grow. Females also produce a small amount of testosterone along with much estrogen. If a female does develop antlers, as sometimes happens, it is because, for some reason, their glands manufactured an extra amount of male sex hormone.

Hormones Control Breeding

The mating season in deer is also under the control of hormones. One of the first signs that rut is about to begin

Whitetail bucks when fighting sometimes get their antlers locked together. Unable to pull apart or feed normally in such a situation, they starve to death.

is the loss of velvet. Bucks scratch at their itchy antlers, sometimes using their hind legs.

When more testosterone appears in the bloodstream, males begin to feel the urge to fight. Soon they are "shadowboxing" every day, swishing the antlers against bushes and saplings. Sometimes young trees are gashed and torn down by these mock fights between bucks and trees.

Bucks threaten rivals and fight when the amount of

testosterone reaches a peak. In a fight one male usually gives up before long, but injury may occur. The writer-photographer Leonard Lee Rue III explains how deer antlers sometimes become locked and thus cause the death of both animals: when the two males first strike their heads together they may hit head-on with such force that the antlers are spread apart for an instant. If one antler slips past and is caught on another when this happens, there is no way the bucks can spread their antlers apart again and become separated.

Does come in heat when there is much estrogen in the bloodstream. This happens about two times during the breeding season. Each period lasts around 24 hours.

Scent glands are between the toes and on the inside of the lower legs. They are influenced by sex hormones and give off especially strong odors at breeding time. Bucks often look for females by trailing them with noses to the ground. Most mating takes place between mid-November and mid-December.

Do Not Pet Fawns!

Does only a year old usually give birth to a single fawn, but afterward they often have twins or perhaps triplets. Quadruplets sometimes appear, and quintuplets have been reported, but these are quite rare. Fawns, like most young mammals, are full of tricks. They run and jump, butt, and leap over each other, chase butterflies and grasshoppers, and sometimes have mock fights that last only an instant. Young females generally stay with their mothers for two years, but young bucks start growing spikes during their second year, and take off on their own.

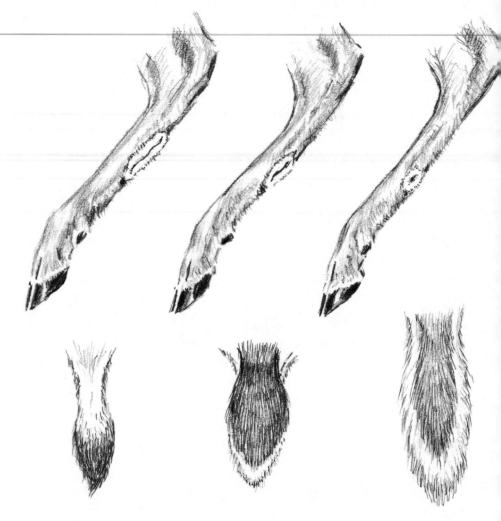

Scent glands and tails of three species of deer (from left to right: mule deer, blacktail, whitetail). Scent glands occur between the toes as well as on the legs.

Young fawns have no scent that can attract enemies, and are left alone by their mothers except when she returns to nurse them. If they are discovered they should not be petted or touched, for the human odor may remain on their fur and draw predators to them. They should never be "rescued." The mother may not be in sight, but she is nearby keeping an eye on the fawn, and will go back to care for it when it is alone.

Deer Diets

Probably one reason whitetails are so widespread is their willingness to eat almost any kind of plant. Among wild foods, acorns are favorites. Deer especially like those of the white oak, which are less bitter than most others. In some areas deer cause great losses to farmers by raiding gardens and crops. They seem to be particularly fond of juicy vegetables and fruits such as celery, cabbage, and apples.

All plant-eating animals need extra minerals and are likely to lick anything with a salty taste. Deer-watchers often use apples or salt blocks as bait to attract deer close enough for study or for photographs. It is strictly against the law, however, for hunters to use bait of any kind to tempt deer closer. "Jacking," or dazzling the animals with the glare of bright lights, is also illegal.

An important winter food of deer is white cedar, but red cedar is a poor food. Deer also feed on other evergreens, dry leaves, and mosses. Although whitetails usually live alone, when snow covers the ground they come together in small bands led by an old doe.

The slender, dainty feet of these animals are not of much use in pawing snow, so they depend on browse. As the groups of animals mill about, feeding on one bush or tree, then another, the snow beneath their feet becomes packed. Soon close networks of trails, or "yards," are formed, over which the animals travel to reach their food supply. They are not likely to leave these shelters even if browse becomes scarce.

Forest Damage

Sometimes forests are severely damaged, especially if there are too many deer. Saplings may be destroyed and older trees killed if bark is eaten. Damage is not limited to the winter season. Bucks in rut often tear up young trees and bushes. Small trees newly set out are especially attractive as food. Deer sometimes eat every young shoot foresters have planted, and seem at times to wait around for more.

Remedies to keep deer away from young plants range from scarecrows to mothballs, but most are useless. Wildlife experts at the New York Botanical Garden are testing a new repellent that seems to work. The "new" substance is a fist-sized ball of human hair tied in nylon net and hung on a branch. Deer will go no closer to the branch than about their own body length. Scientists are now trying to find out just what it is the deer do not like about the hair.

"Toy" Deer

There seems to be some difference in the size of white-tails according to how far north or south they live. The northern race, found in eastern Canada, is larger than the Virginia deer, while Florida whitetails and the Coues deer of the Arizona desert are smaller. Miniature deer of Florida's lower keys are the smallest deer of North America. They stand about as tall as a collie, and weigh somewhat less.

About the time of World War II these beautiful crea-

The little key deer of Florida were almost brought to extinction by motorists, hunters, land developers, and fires.

tures were in danger of extinction. Speeding cars, and fires in the pine and palmetto woods had killed many. Real estate developers took over more and more of the land. Hunters used dogs to flush them from cover then shot the terrified deer as they tried to swim to another island.

By 1947 only about 30 key deer were left, and Gary Allen, an 11-year-old boy, decided to do something about it. He wrote letters to President Truman and, later, to President Eisenhower. He also wrote senators, congressmen, and newspaper editors.

Others joined him. Within a few years letters began to pour in to Congress from all over the United States. Finally laws were passed to give the animals complete protection. In 1963 the Key Deer National Wildlife Refuge was set up.

All this had been started by one small boy who believed in a dream and worked to make that dream come true. Today over 600 key deer live in the refuge and on 18 islands of the lower keys. In the World Wildlife records they are now listed as "Out of danger."

Rocky Mountain Mule Deer

The common deer of our western National Parks is a closely related species, usually called mule deer because of their extremely large ears. The animals are sometimes known in Canada as jumping deer because of their habit, when startled, of bounding away in high, stiff-legged leaps. This species is found in mountains and foothills from the "tail" of Alaska and the Yukon Territory southward into Mexico.

Mule deer (*Odocoileus hemionus*) are larger and stockier than whitetails, and have shorter, less brushy tails. The upper side of the tail may be either white or brown but is always black-tipped. Mule deer tails droop downward, and are often swished from side to side, but are never held erect.

Antlers of the two species are even more different. In mule deer each antler gives off a short spike, then branches equally to form a Y-shaped fork. Later each fork again divides in the same way so that an antler of a mature buck has four equal tines, all pointing upward.

Mule deer are found in small groups more often than are whitetails. In the summer they migrate to higher, cooler mountain valleys, with bucks usually going highest. When winter begins they drift downward. During winter months it is not unusual to see small mixed bands of bucks and does feeding near wapiti and pronghorns. Unlike whitetails, mule deer rarely go near farms and towns.

One well known race of this species, black-tailed deer, is found in forested mountain areas along the Pacific coast. These animals are slightly smaller than mule deer, and the topside of the tail is completely dark. Another race is on the endangered species list. These blacktails live on Cedros Island off the coast of lower California. The Mexican Wildlife Service reported that in 1972 only seven of the deer were seen.

9

Starving, Hunting, Protecting: Problems of Deer and People

Almost since the beginning of time, human beings have interfered with nature in one way or another. Very often the result is disaster. One of the best examples of this is found in the story of the Kaibab mule deer.

During the nineteenth century there were no United States laws controlling hunting, and flesh and skins of deer, wapiti, and moose were sold regularly at market. By 1900, deer were scarce in every state. In the entire country only about 500,000 whitetails were left, and mule deer were gone except for a few scattered populations. One good herd remained. About 4000 Rocky Mountain mule deer lived on the Kaibab Plateau in northern Arizona.

The plateau stretched all along the northern rim of the Grand Canyon. A forest of pine, fir, and spruce sheltered mountain lions and bobcats, coyotes and timber wolves, and the finest deer herd in the United States. For centuries the animals had lived there in perfect balance.

President Theodore Roosevelt wanted to be sure this fine herd was saved. In 1906 he created the Grand Canyon Game Preserve and made the plateau the special home of the deer. He also gave orders to the newly formed Forest Service to see that the deer were protected from enemies, and could breed.

First, all hunting was outlawed. Next, war was declared on all predators. Wolves were wiped out. Coyotes, mountain lions, and bobcats could not be destroyed completely, but all that were left were shot on sight.

By 1918 the herd had doubled, then redoubled. Almost no predators were left that could rid the herd of the sick, the crippled, and other misfits. Numbers had now reached nearly 16,000. Some of the better grasses had disappeared and many trees and bushes were damaged.

There was no longer good food for all the deer. Forest supervisors warned there would be trouble ahead unless they were allowed to make some changes in management. For the next several years officials did little except argue about what should be done.

Disaster!

By 1924 the herd numbered close to 100,000. Zane Grey, a novelist, suggested that Arizona cowboys round up several thousand deer and herd them off the plateau and onto good range. The drive began, but failed. It is almost impossible to drive wild deer. Animals that were flushed out dodged back and forth in all directions, and hid in thickets. When a way opened up they raced back behind the cowboys to safety. The plateau was their home, and they were going to stay there.

During the next few winters thousands starved and froze. Trees in the forest were stripped of every leaf and twig as high as deer could reach. Animals that remained alive were weak, skinny, and sick, full of parasites their bodies had not the strength to fight.

After many bitter arguments the Supreme Court ruled in 1928 that the Forest Service was in charge of Federal lands, and had the right and the responsibility to set up and enforce rules that would protect the land, plants, and animals in their charge. Plans were made, and work began. However, over a quarter of a century passed before recovery was well on the way.

To Hunt or Not to Hunt

Animals and plants on the Kaibab Plateau are now healthy and not overcrowded, but the balance is an artificial one. The deer are kept in check by the use of several kinds of hunts. For example, when there are too many does, the Preserve is opened for "antlerless hunts." Sometimes hunters are allowed to choose whether they will kill bucks or does. On other hunts more than one animal can be taken.

Natural balance could be set up again only if natural predators were brought back into the forest. This was not tried because part of the land on the plateau was leased to ranchers. Thousands of sheep and hundreds of cattle and horses fed there. Sheepmen and cattlemen feared that hungry coyotes or bobcats might take lambs or calves instead of fawns, and the government agreed to follow their wishes.

Deer, like other hoofed animals that serve as food for predators, are in some ways their own worst enemies. They are so fertile that if conditions are at all good, their number shoots up quickly. In a few years they can "eat themselves out of house and home," and often become a nuisance to the countryside. To many people the only answer to this problem is to have a longer hunting season.

One argument for this points to human history. Primitive peoples today, and for as far back as we have any kind of record, are and have been hunter-gatherers. Men hunted. Women and children gathered roots, berries, nuts, and other such foods. Because men have hunted for thousands

Blacktails, or other species, in large numbers can eat in a given area till they have cleared away every available bit of food. Note the "browse lines" on the trees in the background, stripped of edible bark as high as the deer can reach.

of years there are many today who say hunting is an instinctive thing in men. Such an argument should apply to women also, but nobody suggests that women are seized each fall with an instinctive desire to go to the woods to hunt roots, nuts, and other wild foods.

Whatever the arguments for or against hunting, there

are a great many people for whom hunting is part of their way of life. This is a fact that, at present, has to be accepted. It is also a fact that millions of dollars in hunting fees and taxes, which we would not otherwise have, are used for wildlife management.

A Few Changes Are Needed

However, there is room for improvement. Too often such money has not been wisely spent. Some regulations favor big game at the expense of other animal and plant life. Many times rules and laws are not even in the best interest of the favored big game animals themselves.

One needed change is a prohibition against unnecessary cruelty to animals. Instant death by a rifle shot is far better than a lingering death by starvation, but not all shots kill cleanly. Many agonizing deaths are caused by a certain class of "sportsmen" who are "out for fun." They hold licenses, but have never bothered to learn to stalk and shoot properly, or to take care of guns or game. They follow few rules except their own whims.

When one drives a car, certain rules apply. A person is given a license only after he has proved by actual test he is able to drive a car sensibly and safely, and after he has passed a test on his knowledge of safety rules and traffic regulations. If laws are broken he may be fined or have his license taken away. These controls do not stop all accidents and deaths with cars, but they help.

The same sort of thing might well be required for hunters. One who is really interested in hunting, and who wants it to be an activity that is respected, would agree that a person with a license to hunt should be skillful in handling a gun, and should *know* and be willing to abide by—not just have read through—the Ten Commandments of Hunting Safety that sports organizations publish. A hunting license, like a driving license, should be allowed only to those who have shown they deserve to hold it. An increase in the fees connected with hunting licenses could pay for the expense involved.

Wildlife is part of our heritage. It is also part of our need for a full and satisfying life. We are stewards and care-takers of the living things that share the earth with us; we should not be rulers and tyrants over them. Deer, moose, bears, wolves, skunks, and mice all have their own special niche to fill in the wilderness. We properly fill our niche on the earth not by destroying other things, but by respecting and enjoying them on nature's terms.

Suggested Reading

Books

Burton, Maurice, and Robert Burton, eds., *International Wildlife Encyclopedia* (20 vols., Marshall Cavendish, New York, 1970)

Cahalane, Victor H., *Mammals of North America* (Macmillan, New York, 1961)

Caras, Roger, *North American Mammals, Fur-Bearing Animals of the United States and Canada* (Galahad Books, Division of A.&W. Promotional Book Corporation, New York, 1967)

Crandall, Lee S., *The Management of Wild Mammals in Captivity* (University of Chicago Press, Chicago, 1964)

———, *A Zoo Man's Notebook* (University of Chicago Press, Chicago, 1966; Père David's deer)

Grzimek, Bernhard, ed., *Animal Life Encyclopedia*, vol. 13 (Van Nostrand Reinhold, New York, 1972)

Hopf, Alice L., *Biography of an American Reindeer* (Putnam, New York, 1976)

Kurtén, Björn, *The Ice Age* (Putnam, New York, 1972)

Prideaux, Tom, and Editors of Time-Life Books, *Cro-Magnon Man* (Time-Life Books, New York, 1973)

Rue, Leonard Lee, III, *The World of the White-Tailed Deer* (Lippincott, Philadelphia, 1962)

———, *The Deer of North America* (Crown, New York, 1979)

Ryden, Hope, *The Little Deer of the Florida Keys* (Putnam, New York, 1978)

Sanderson, Ivan T., *Living Mammals of the World* (Doubleday, Garden City, New York, 1972)

Schaller, George B., *The Deer and the Tiger: A Study of Wildlife in India* (University of Chicago Press, Chicago, 1967)

Van Wormer, Joe, *The World of the American Elk* (Lippincott, Philadelphia, 1969)

——, *The World of the Moose* (Lippincott, Philadelphia, 1972)

Magazine Articles

Algard, Goran, "Lapland's Reindeer Roundup" (*National Geographic*, July 1949)

Allen, Durward L. and L. David Mech, "Wolves Versus Moose on Isle Royale" (*National Geographic*, February 1963)

Allen, Robert P., "Can We Save the Key Deer?" (*Natural History*, February 1951)

Anderson, Sally, "Norway's Reindeer Lapps" (*National Geographic*, September 1977)

Bailey, Vernon, "Our Noblest Deer, the American Elk or Wapiti" (*Nature Magazine*, September 1937)

Davis, Raymond 'Sandy,' "Hope for Western White-Tail" (*Defenders*, December 1976)

Edmiston, Beula, "Sanctuary for the Tule Elk" (*National Parks and Conservation Magazine*, June 1972)

Gould, Stephen Jay, "The Misnamed, Mistreated, Misunderstood Irish Elk" (*Natural History*, March 1973)

Haas, George H., "What's In a Name?" (*National Wildlife*, December-January 1977)

Hamer, Allegra, "Père David's Deer" (*Animal Kingdom*, February-March 1974)

Harris, Jennie E., "His Perfume Stirs the World" (*Natural History*, February 1947)

Heinhold, George, "Elk, Sultans of the Rockies" (*Science Digest*, May 1971)

Helgeland, Glenn, "Get Out on a Limb" (*National Wildlife*, August-September 1977; deer-watching)

Kelsall, John P., "Migration of the Barren-Ground Caribou" (*Natural History*, January 1970)

MacNamara, Mark C., "Dwarf Deer of the Andes" (*Animal Kingdom*, June-July 1978)

Modell, Walter, "Horns and Antlers" (*Scientific American,* April 1969)

National Parks Magazine, "Issue: Tule Elk" (April 1969)

Petite, Irving, "A Black-tailed Deer Comes of Age" (*Audubon,* January-February 1958)

Rearden, Jim, "Caribou: Hardy Nomads of the North" (*National Geographic,* December 1974)

Schaller, George B., "Countdown for Marsh Deer" (*Animal Kingdom,* June-July 1978)

Science Digest, "Too Many Deer?" (January 1970)

Scott, Jack Denton, "The Durable Deer" (*Reader's Digest,* December 1969)

———, "His Magnificence, the Moose" (*Reader's Digest,* October 1965) (Also in *National Wildlife,* October-November 1965)

Trefethen, James B., "The Terrible Lesson of the Kaibab" (*National Wildlife,* June-July 1967)

Wilhelm, Eugene J., Jr., "Return of the Elk to Appalachia" (*National Parks Magazine,* January 1967)

Index